Student Note-Taking Guide to accompany

Managing Stress

*Principles and Strategies
for Health and Well-Being*

Fifth Edition

Brian Luke Seaward

JONES AND BARTLETT PUBLISHERS

Sudbury, Massachusetts

BOSTON   TORONTO   LONDON   SINGAPORE

World Headquarters
Jones and Bartlett Publishers
40 Tall Pine Drive
Sudbury, MA 01776
978-443-5000
info@jbpub.com
www.jbpub.com   06/09

Jones and Bartlett Publishers Canada
6339 Ormindale Way
Mississauga, ON L5V 1J2
CANADA

Jones and Bartlett Publishers International
Barb House, Barb Mews
London W6 7PA
UK

ISBN: 0-7637-3847-6

Cover Image: © Image Source/Getty Images

Printed in the United States of America
09 08 07 06 05   10 9 8 7 6 5 4 3 2 1

Contents

How This Book Can Help You Learn

All of us have different learning styles. Some of us are visual learners, some more auditory, some learn better by doing an activity. Some students prefer to learn new material using visual aids. Some learn material better when they hear it in a lecture; others learn it better by reading it. Cognitive research has shown that no matter what your learning style, you will learn more if you are actively engaged in the learning process.

This Student Note-Taking Guide will help you learn by providing a structure to your notes and letting you utilize all of the learning styles mentioned above. Students don't need to copy down every word their professor says or recopy their entire textbook. Do the assigned reading, listen in lecture, follow the key points your instructor is making, and write down meaningful notes. After reading and lectures, review your notes and pull out the most important points.

The Student Note-Taking Guide is your partner and guide in note-taking. Your Guide provides you with a visual guide that follows the chapter topics presented in your textbook. If your instructor is using the PowerPoint slides that accompany the text, this guide will save you from having to write down everything that is on the slides. There is space provided for you to jot down the terms and concepts that you feel are most important to each lecture. By working with your Guide, you are seeing, hearing, writing, and, later, reading and reviewing. The more often you are exposed to the material, the better you will learn and understand it. Using different methods of exposure significantly increases your comprehension.

Your Guide is the perfect place to write down questions that you want to ask your professor later, interesting ideas that you want to discuss with your study group, or reminders to yourself to go back and study a certain concept again to make sure that you really got it.

Having organized notes is essential at exam time and when doing homework assignments. Your ability to easily locate the important concepts of a recent lecture will help you move along more rapidly, as you don't have to spend time rereading an entire chapter just to reinforce one point that you may not have quite understood.

Your Guide is a valuable resource. You've found a wonderful study partner!

Note-Taking Tips

1. It is easier to take notes if you are not hearing the information for the first time. Read the chapter or the material that is about to be discussed before class. This will help you to anticipate what will be said in class, and have an idea of what to write down. It will also help to read over your notes from the last class. This way you can avoid having to spend the first few minutes of class trying to remember where you left off last time.

2. Don't waste your time trying to write down everything that your professor says. Instead, listen closely and only write down the important points. Review these important points after class to help remind you of related points that were made during the lecture.

3. If the class discussion takes a spontaneous turn, pay attention and participate in the discussion. Only take notes on the conclusions that are relevant to the lecture.

4. Emphasize main points in your notes. You may want to use a highlighter, special notation (asterisks, exclamation points), format (circle, underline), or placement on the page (indented, bulleted). You will find that when you try to recall these points, you will be able to actually picture them on the page.

5. Be sure to copy down word-for-word specific formulas, laws, and theories.

6. Hearing something repeated, stressed, or summed up can be a signal that it is an important concept to understand.

7. Organize handouts, study guides, and exams in your notebook along with your lecture notes. It may be helpful to use a three-ring binder, so that you can insert pages wherever you need to.

8. When taking notes, you might find it helpful to leave a wide margin on all four sides of the page. Doing this allows you to note names, dates, definitions, etc., for easy access and studying later. It may also be helpful to make notes of questions you want to ask your professor about or research later, ideas or relationships that you want to explore more on your own, or concepts that you don't fully understand.

9. It is best to maintain a separate notebook for each class. Labeling and dating your notes can be helpful when you need to look up information from previous lectures.

10. Make your notes legible, and take notes directly in your notebook. Chances are you won't recopy them no matter how noble your intentions. Spend the time you would have spent recopying the notes studying them instead, drawing conclusions and making connections that you didn't have time for in class.

11. Look over your notes after class while the lecture is still fresh in your mind. Fix illegible items and clarify anything you don't understand. Do this again right before the next class.

Notes

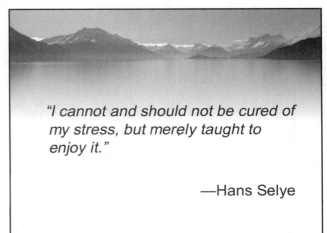

The Nature of Stress

- Around 1960 Hans Selye proposed that stress is part of the human condition

- About 1990 the World Health Organization calls stress "a global epidemic"

- By the turn of the 21st century, stress has clearly become a way of life, although not necessary a good one

The Nature of 21st Century Stress

- A 24-7 society where everything and everyone is accessible all the time
- The rapid rate of change, from technology to economics to family dynamics
- Growing threat of terrorism, global warming, other changing world dynamics
- Greater responsibilities and seemingly less freedom
- The number of stressors in our lives appears to be increasing
- The amount of leisure time appears to be decreasing

A Question of Poor Boundaries

- Poor boundaries are a big issue that tend to undermine our lives
- People have poor boundaries, thus adding fuel to the stress fire
- Boundaries between work and home
- Boundaries between technology and privacy
- Financial boundaries (massive credit card debt)
- Poor boundaries with television, Internet, food, relationships, etc.

A Question of Poor Boundaries
(continued)

- Poor boundaries tend to be violated (making you feel like you are being walked over), hence making you feel victimized; another way to describe stress.

- As the saying goes: Once a victim, twice a volunteer. Learn from your experiences and strengthen you personal boundaries as needed so you don't fall prey to "victim consciousness."

The Nature of 21st Century Stress II

- Research now indicates a solid link between lifestyles and stress-related disease.

- As much as 70–85% of all disease and illness is stress-related, from the common cold to cancer, from herpes to hemorrhoids.

The Many Faces of Stress

- Because of the combinations of stressors, one's personality, and one's life experiences, stress becomes a complicated phenomenon. Despite these factors, the many means to cope with stress offer strategies for all these factors.

Notes

Popular Views of Stress

- Eastern philosophies have viewed stress as "an absence of inner peace."

- Western culture has more recently viewed stress as "a loss of control."

- It is also viewed as an inability to cope with problems.

Definitions of Stress

- Definitions of stress are often based on various disciplines of study (e.g., psychology, physiology, sociology, anthropology, theology, etc.)
- Consequently there are many different definitions of stress (e.g., loss of emotional control, wear and tear on the body, an inability to cope, an absence of inner peace)

Richard Lazarus' View of Stress

- Stress is a state of anxiety produced when events and responsibilities exceed one's coping abilities.

Hans Selye's View of Stress

- Stress is the nonspecific response of the body to any demand placed upon it to adapt, whether that demand produces pleasure or pain.

A Holistic Medicine View of Stress

- Stress is the inability to cope with a perceived or real (or imagined) threat to one's mental, physical, emotional, and spiritual well-being, which results in a series of physiological responses and adaptations.

The Stress Response (Fight-or-Flight Response)

- Introduced by Walter Cannon in 1914
- A survival instinct to fight or run
- Meant for physical stressors (e.g., running from a burning building)
- It appears not to be meant for non-physical stressors such as never-ending traffic, unruly mother-in-laws or the roommate from hell

Notes

The Stress Response
(Fight-or-Flight Response)
(continued)

- Arousal also happens for nonphysical stressors (mental, emotional, and spiritual).
- No matter if the threat is real (car accident) or perceived (a noise at night), the stress response occurs.
- The stress response occurs in proportion to the perceived danger.

Stages of the Stress Response

- Stage 1: Stimuli received by brain through one or more of five senses.
- Stage 2: Brain deciphers stimuli (either a threat or as a non-threat)
- Stage 3: Body stays aroused until threat is over.
- Stage 4: Body returns to homeostasis once the threat is gone.

Symptoms of Fight or Flight

- Increased heart rate
- Increased blood rate
- Increased ventilation
- Vasodilatation of arteries to body's periphery (arm and legs)
- Increased serum glucose levels

Symptoms of Fight or Flight
(continued)

- Increased free fatty acid mobilization
- Increased blood coagulation and decreased clotting
- Increased muscular strength
- Decreased gastric movement
- Increased perspiration to cool body core temperature

Tend and Befriend Theory

- Theory introduced by Shelly Taylor and colleagues in 2000
- Women have a second stress response: Connectedness (an effective coping skill)
- Taylor believes it is hardwired into women's DNA, and revealed through hormones
- It has also been referred to as "nest and nurture"
- Women still will fight or flee, if need be

Stress and Insomnia

- Estimates suggest that over 60% of Americans are sleep deprived.

- Emotional stress is thought to be the primary cause of insomnia.

- "Sleep stealers" also include menopause, jet lag, caffeine, shift work, meds, repeated cell phone use.

Stress and Insomnia
(continued)

Improved "sleep hygiene" habits include:
- Meditation
- Minimize/avoid caffeine after 6:00 p.m.
- Engage in a regular fitness program
- Keep a regular sleep cycle
  (regular circadian rhythms)

Stress and Insomnia
(continued)

Improved "sleep hygiene" habits include:

- Create and maintain a sleep-friendly environment (e.g., room temperature and darkness).
- Avoid watching television before bedtime.
- Minimize/avoid evening cell phone use.

Stress and Insomnia
(continued)

Remember this:

Sleep is not recognized as an effective relaxation technique due to the procession of unconscious thoughts (dreams) that can trigger the stress response while sleeping.

Three Types of Stress

1. Eustress: good stress (e.g., falling in love)
2. Neustress: neutral stress (e.g., earthquake in remote corner of world)
3. Distress: bad stress (e.g., death of a close friend); acute stress (high intensity, short duration); chronic stress* (low intensity, prolonged time)

* Seems to cause the most problems with disease and illness

Three Types of Stressors

1. Bio-ecological Influences
   (e.g., solar flares, SAD, ELFs, GMOs)
2. Psychointrapersonal Influences
   (e.g., relationships, self-esteem, ego, etc.)
3. Social Influences
   (e.g., urban sprawl, traffic, politics, etc.)

Stress in a Changing World

- Technostress
- College Stress
- Occupational Stress
- Seniors: The Stress of Aging

Notes

Notes

Stress in a Changing World
(continued)

Technostress
- Poor boundaries
- Privacy issues
- Ethical issues
- Compromised family time
- Computer dating?
- Outdated software

Stress in a Changing World
(continued)

College Stress
- Living conditions (roommate "from hell")
- Professional pursuits
- Academic deadlines
- Financial problems (loans)
- Lifestyle behaviors
- Sexuality/intimacy issues

Stress in a Changing World
(continued)

Occupational Stress
- Commuting/traffic
- Working conditions (The boss "from hell")
- Clients/customers "from hell"
- Lack of good benefits
- Lack of employer loyalty
- Job security issues

Stress in a Changing World
(continued)

Stress and the Retired Population
- Financial security issues
- Social support issues
- Health issues
- Medicare, Social Security issues
- Raising grandkids

Wellness Paradigm

- Spiritual well-being
- Emotional well-being

- Mental (intellectual) well-being
- Physical well-being

Wellness Paradigm
(continued)

- The integration, balance, and harmony of the mind, body, spirit, and emotions for optimal well-being, where the whole is considered greater than the sum of the parts.

Notes

Notes

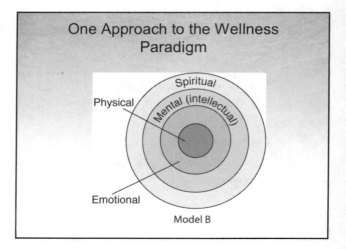

One Approach to the Wellness Paradigm

Spiritual

Physical

Mental (intellectual)

Emotional

Model B

A Holistic Approach to
Stress Management

- To deal effectively with stress, all areas
  must be addressed equally to integrate,
  balance, and give harmony for optimal
  well-being

An Effective Holistic Approach to
Stress Management Includes:

- Physical well-being, the ability of all the
  body's physiological systems to function
  optimally
- Mental well-being, ability to gather,
  process, recall, and communicate
  information

An Effective Holistic Approach to Stress Management (continued)

- Emotional well-being, ability to recognize, feel, and control the entire range of human emotions
- Spiritual well-being, the evolution of higher consciousness through relationships, values, and purpose in life

What Is Holistic Stress Management?

- To live in the present moment
- To integrate, balance, and harmonize all aspects of mind, body, spirit, and emotions
- To move from a motivation of fear to a motivation of love/compassion
- To unite the conscious and unconscious minds
- To balance the power of ego with the purpose of soul

"I'm an old man now, and I've known a great many problems in my life, most of which never happened."

—Mark Twain

Notes

_____

_____

_____

_____

_____

_____

_____

_____

_____

_____

_____

_____

_____

_____

_____

_____

_____

_____

_____

_____

_____

_____

_____

_____

_____

_____

_____

_____

_____

_____

_____

_____

_____

_____

_____

"If you're looking for fast acting relief, try slowing down."

—Lily Tomlin

Study Guide Questions

1. How would you best define stress?

2. How does acute stress differ from chronic stress?

3. What is the General Adaptation Syndrome? List the stages.

Study Guide Questions
(continued)

4. Do men and women respond to stress the same way? Please explain.

5. How does stress effect sleep? List as many ways as possible (including sleep stealers).

6. What is holistic stress management?

Notes

Managing
Stress
*Principles and Strategies
for Health and Well-Being*

The Physiology of Stress

Chapter 2

"To understand the stress response, we must process a fundamental knowledge not only of psychology but of physiology as well."

—George Everly

The Physiology of Stress

- A series of neural and chemical reactions meant for physical survival

- If you can begin to understand the physiology of stress, then you can begin to use this knowledge to augment your own health and well-being in terms of techniques like mental imagery, biofeedback, diaphragmatic breathing, etc.

The Physiology of Stress
(continued)

- Hans Selye, considered by many as the father of the study of stress, developed the idea that a direct relationship exists between chronic stress and excessive wear and tear throughout the body.

Psychophysiology

- *Psychophysiology* is a term to describe the body's physiological reaction to perceived stressors suggesting that the stress response is a mind-body phenomenon.

The Human Brain

Divided into three levels:

1. The vegetative level
   Autonomic responses
   (e.g., breathing, heart rate, etc.)

2. The limbic system
   Emotional thought processing

3. The neocortical level
   Human consciousness
   (rational thought processing)

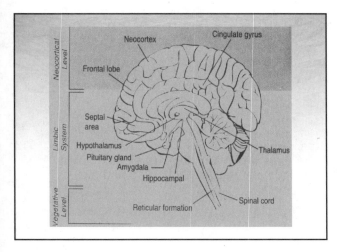

The Nervous System Can Be Divided Into:

- The central nervous system (CNS)
  - brain
  - spinal cord
- The peripheral nervous system (PNS)
  - consists of all neural pathways to the extremities

The Vegetative Level

- The lowest level of the brain is comprised of the:
  - reticular formation
  - brain stem

Reticular Activating System (RAS)

- The RAS is the link connecting the brain to the spinal cord.
- Several stress physiologists believe that this is the bridge joining the mind and the body as one.
- This organ functions as a communication link between the mind and the body.

The Brain Stem

- The brain stem, comprised of the pons, medulla oblongata, and mesencephalon, is responsible for involuntary functions of the human body such as:
  - heartbeat
  - respiration
  - vasomotor activity

The Limbic System

- The limbic system is the emotional control center and comprised of the:
  - thalamus
  - hypothalamus
  - pituitary gland (also known as the *master endocrine gland*)
- These three glands work in unison to maintain a level of homeostasis

The Neocortical Level

- The neocortex is the highest level of the brain.
- It is at this level that sensory information is processed as a threat or a non-threat and where cognition takes place.
- This higher level of the brain can override a lower level and can influence emotional responses.

Physiological Systems Involved in the Stress Response

- The nervous system

- The endocrine system

- The immune system

The Autonomic Nervous System (ANS)

- The ANS regulates visceral activities and vital organs, including:
  - circulation
  - digestion
  - respiration
  - temperature regulation

Two Branches of the ANS That Act to Maintain Homeostatic Balance

- Sympathetic Nervous System

- Parasympathetic Nervous System

Sympathetic Nervous System

- Is responsible for the responses associated with the fight-or-flight response
- This physical arousal is stimulated through the release of catecholamines
  - epinephrine (adrenaline)
  - norepinephrine (noradrenaline)

Parasympathetic Nervous System

- Maintains homeostasis through the release of acetylcholine (ACh)
- Is responsible for energy conservation and relaxation

The Endocrine System

- Consists of a series of hormonal glands located throughout the body which regulate metabolic functions that require endurance rather than speed
- The endocrine system is a network of four components:
  - glands, hormones, circulation, and target organs

The Endocrine System
(continued)

- The glands most closely involved with the stress response are the:
  - pituitary
  - thyroid
  - adrenal

The Nervous System and the Endocrine System

- Join together to form metabolic pathways or axis
- There are three pathways:
  - the ACTH axis
  - the vasopressin axis
  - the thyroxine axis

Notes

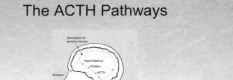

The ACTH Pathways

Three Stages of Effects Associated with the Stress Response

- Immediate effects of stress
- Intermediate effects of stress
- Prolonged effects of stress

Immediate Effects of Stress

- Sympathetic nervous response
- Epinephrine and norepinephrine released
- Time: 2 to 3 seconds
- Like a phone call or instant message

Intermediate Effects of Stress

- Adrenal response
- Epinephrine and norepinephrine release from adrenal medulla
- Time: 20 to 30 seconds
- Like an email

Prolonged Effects of Stress

- ACTH, vasopressin, and thyroxine affect various metabolic processes
- Time: minutes, hours, days, or weeks
- Like an "overnight delivery"

Immediate, Intermediate, and Prolonged Effects of Stress

Immediate effects	Intermediate effects	Prolonged effects
Phone call	Email	Overnight delivery

Notes

_____

Other Stress-Related Hormones

- DHEA

- Serotonin

- Melatonin

A Decade of Brain Research
(1992–2002)

- Use of MRIs to measure conscious thoughts
- Repeated exposure to cortisol increases aging process of brain
- Repeated exposure to cortisol damages/ shrinks brain tissue
- Damage due to repeated exposure to cortisol appears to be irreversible
- We are "wired for stress" for physical threats yet all threats set the alarm

Insomnia and Brain Physiology

- Various neurochemicals are released in the brain during episodes of stress that can greatly affect one's quality of sleep.

- The brain chemistry equation for sleep involves many neurochemicals including a delicate balance between seratonin and melatonin.

Insomnia and Brain Physiology
(continued)

- As daylight decreases, melatonin levels increase to help promote sleep.

- Various factors affect seratonin levels, including light, food chemistry (carbohydrates), pharmaceutical use, and emotional stress, which in turn affect melatonin levels and hence the quality of sleep.

Study Guide Questions

1. What role does the nervous system play in the stress response?

2. What role does the endocrine system play in the stress response?

3. Name the three pathways (axes) of stress physiology.

4. What does new brain imaging tell us about stress physiology?

Chapter 3: Stress and Disease

Notes

_____
_____
_____
_____
_____
_____
_____
_____
_____
_____
_____
_____
_____
_____
_____
_____
_____
_____
_____
_____
_____
_____
_____
_____
_____
_____
_____
_____
_____
_____
_____
_____
_____
_____
_____
_____
_____
_____
_____

Managing Stress
Principles and Strategies
for Health and Well-Being

Stress and Disease

Chapter 3

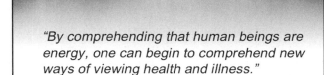

"By comprehending that human beings are energy, one can begin to comprehend new ways of viewing health and illness."

—Richard Gerber, M.D.

The Nature of Disease and Illness: A Little History

- Western medicine was forged by the Cartesian Principle
- Louis Pasteur: All diseases are the cause of microbes. This later became known as "The Germ Theory"
- Claude Bernard: Disease manifests in a poor environment ranging from poor eating habits to emotional distress
- Western medicine never bought into Bernard's theory
- In the 1930s the term _psychosomatic_ was coined to describe diseases and illnesses precipitated by mental/emotional aspects

The Nature of Disease and Illness

- Western science has not been able to fully demonstrate a concrete connection between stress and disease, though closer steps are slowly being made in mind-body medicine

Stress and Disease Connection

- Roughly 80% of all doctor's office visits are related to stress

- Current research indicates that between 70% and 80% of all health-related problems are either precipitated or aggravated by emotional stress (e.g., type II diabetes, colds, flu, migraines, lupus, cancer, etc.)

"The body is the battlefield for the war games of the mind."

—Brian Luke Seaward

The Dynamics Between Stress and Disease

- To understand the relationship between stress and disease, one needs to understand that several factors act in unison to create a pathological outcome including:

  - Cognitive perceptions of a threatening stimuli
  - Activation of the sympathetic nervous system
  - Engagement of the endocrine system
  - Engagement of the immune system

Psychoneuroimmunology

- A term coined by Robert Ader around 1980 to explain the integrative dynamics of mind and body
- Pelletier defines psychoneuroimmunology as the study of the intricate interaction of consciousness (psycho), brain and central nervous system (neuro), and body's defense against external infection and internal aberrant cell division (immunology)

Changing Paradigms in Health and Disease

- While today there are many who still ascribe to the Germ Theory (and variations of it with DNA defects), new research continues to reveal that the biomedical model of health and disease is incomplete.

- Research into various forms of complementary and alternative medicine (CAM) reveal that the dynamics of illness and healing cannot be confined to the biomedical model (the body is a machine with parts to be fixed or replaced).

- The body is not comprised of many physiological systems, it's one system!

Notes

Four Theoretical Models

- The Borysenko Model (immune system)
- The Pert Model (nervous system)
- The Gerber Model (psycho-mind)
- The Pelletier Premodel (piecing things together)

The Borysenko Model

- Borysenko outlined a dichotomy of stress-induced dysregulation and a matrix describing the immune balance regarding four classifications of diseases.

- "Stress alters the vulnerability of the immune system to both exogenous and endogenous antigens (cortisol destroys white blood cells)."

- Further research reveals that acute psychological stress decreases NK cell activity through a profound effect on cytokine production.

A Brief Exposure to the Immune System

- The immune system is a network of several organs throughout the body (e.g., bone marrow, thymus, spleen).

- Lymphocytes are one of many leukocytes. Most noteworthy are the T-lymphocytes and B-lymphocytes.

- Only about 2% of lymphocytes are in circulation at any one time.

A Brief Exposure to the Immune System
(continued)

The family of leukocytes

- T cytotoxic cells (T-cells that release cytokines)
- T-helpers (CD4)
- T-suppressors (CD8)

Borysenko's Stress and Disease Dichotomy

Autonomic Dysregulation (Overresponsive ANS)	Immune Dysregulation
Migraines	Infection (virus)
Peptic ulcers	Allergies
Irritable bowel syndrome	AIDS
Hypertension	Cancer
Coronary heart disease	Lupus
Asthma	Arthritis

Borysenko's Immune Activity Matrix

	Over-reactions	Under-reactions
Exogenous activity	Allergies	Infections (colds & flu) Herpes Cancer
Endogenous activity	Arthritis Lupus	

Notes

Notes

The Pert Model

- Pert's model, based on her research and others', strongly links the nervous system with the immune system.
- Various cell tissues comprising the immune system can synthesize neuropeptides to alter (- or +) immune function.
- Various cells throughout the body (stomach, spleen, etc.) can also synthesize neuropeptides.
- Positive emotions can enhance immune function ("molecules of emotion").

The Pert Model
(continued)

- The Pert Model is supported and enhanced by other researchers including the work of Kiecolt-Glaser (Ohio State University).
  - Medical students, stress and decreased immune response
  - Stress and the decreased rate of wound healing
  - Stress and the acceleration of the aging process
  - Many other studies on stress neurophysiology

The Pert Model
(continued)

- Whereas before Pert's findings, it was believed that cortisol played the crucial role in immuno-suppression, it is now thought that structural changes in neuropeptides, influenced by emotional thought, play the most significant role in immuno-incompetence.

The Gerber Model

- Gerber's Model uses a holistic approach or systems-theory approach to health.

- The mind is not a series of biochemical reactions in the gray matter of the brain. Rather, the mind is an energy comprised of both conscious and unconscious thoughts, that uses the brain as its primary organ of choice.

- This energy, a subtle energy, surrounds and permeates the body.

The Gerber Model
(continued)

- Changes in energy, through changes in thoughts, affect the physical body.
- Disease is a disturbance in the human energy field, which cascades through the levels of subtle energy to the body, via meridians and chakras.
- Disease doesn't begin in the body, it ends up in the body.
- We don't have a mind in a body, we have a body in the mind.

The Gerber Model (diagram)

Central channel
Physical body
Etheric body
Astral body
Mental body
Causal body

The Gerber Model
(continued)

A brief lesson in Subtle Anatomy:

1. The Human Energy Field
   (the human aura-electromagnetic energy)

2. The meridian energy system
   (based on Chinese medicine)

3. The chakra energy system
   (based on Ayurvedic medicine)

.

The Gerber Model
(continued)

- Stress-related symptoms that appear in the physical body are the manifestation of unresolved issues that have occurred earlier, as a result of disturbances at a higher energy level.

- Thoughts and perceptions and emotions that originate in the various layers of subtle energy cascade through the mind-body interface and are decoded at the molecular level to cause biological changes (disease) in the body.

The Gerber Model
(continued)

- What puzzles health experts is why two people experiencing the same stressor can end up having different illnesses. When looked at though the Gerber Model, based on ageless wisdom of energy healing, perhaps this begins to make more sense.

- Gerber's model is also based on the contemporary work of Carolyn Myss, Donna Eden, Mietek Wirkus, Roslynn Bruere, and others.

- Gerber's Model is now the primary focus of research involving various forms of CAM.

A Brief Lesson on the Chakra System

Chakra	Body Region	Emotional Aspect
1. Crown Chakra	Crown	Spiritual issues
2. Brow Chakra	Head	Cognitive issues
3. Throat Chakra	Thyroid	Self-expression/ Assertiveness

A Brief Lesson on the Chakra System
(continued)

Chakra	Body Region	Emotional Aspect
4. Heart Chakra	Heart	Anger issues
5. Solar Plexus Chakra	Adrenals	Anxiety issues
6. Naval Chakra	GI Tract	Self-esteem issues
7. Root Chakra	Sex Organs	Security issues

Support for the Gerber Model

- Electromagnetic pollution affects one's health
- MRIs are based on electromagnetic energy, quantum physics, and the law of entrainment
- Military design of weapons based on human energy field
- CIA use of remote viewing based on non-local mind
- Scientific studies validate many aspects of Subtle Anatomy

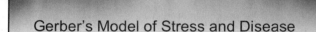

Gerber's Model of Stress and Disease

"Thoughts are particles of energy. (Negative) thoughts are accompanied by emotions which also begin at the energy levels. As these particles of energy filter through from the etheric level to the physical level, the end result is immunoincompetence."

—Richard Gerber, M.D.

The Pelletier Premodel

- In 2003, 15 years after he first created this pre-model, Pelletier stated that the Western medical model is still stuck in the old paradigm, not fully embracing the tenet of mind-body-spirit holism.

- Pelletier believes that a number of issues must be fully addressed and understood before a complete stress and disease model can be understood.

- Facts that fly in the face of the premise that "the body is a machine" and "consciousness is a epiphenomenon of neurochemicals in the brain."

- These phenomena are commonly known as the "Ghost in the Machine."

Ghosts in the Biomedical Model Machine

- These events leave people scratching their "biomedical" heads

  - Multiple Personality Disorder (MPD)
  - Spontaneous remissions (e.g., cancerous tumors, etc.)
  - Placebos and nocebos (belief systems)
  - Cell memory
  - Subtle energy healings and nonlocal prayer healings
  - Immunoenhancement

Conclusion Drawn from Pelletier

- The only logical approach to understanding the stress-disease/mind-body phenomenon is an approach in which the individual is considered greater than the sum of its physiological parts. One must consider the spiritual dimension of health and disease as well.

Target Organs and Their Disorders

- Initially or ultimately one or more organs in the body is the recipient of stress-based neurological and hormonal activity that causes wear and tear, to the point where it no longer functions optimally.
- Disorders, at the present time, appear to fall into two categories:
    - Nervous system disorders
    - Immune system disorders

Nervous System-Related Disorders

- Bronchial asthma
- Tension headaches
- Migraine headaches
- TMJD (temporomandibular joint disorder)
- IBS (irritable bowel syndrome)
- Coronary heart disease

Notes

Immune System-Related Disorders

- The common cold and influenza
- Allergies
- Rheumatoid arthritis
- Ulcers and colitis
- Lupus
- Cancer

Study Guide Questions

1. Describe the Borysenko (immune system) stress and disease model.

2. Describe the Pert (brain neurophysiology) stress and disease model.

3. Describe the Gerber (energy systems) stress and disease model.

Study Guide Questions
(continued)

4. Describe the Pelletier stress and disease model.

5. List five health issues that are nervous system diseases related to stress.

6. List five health issues that are immune system diseases related to stress.

Notes

Managing Stress
Principles and Strategies
for Health and Well-Being

Part 2:

The Mind and Soul

Managing Stress
Principles and Strategies
for Health and Well-Being

Toward a Psychology of Stress

Chapter 4

"Modern man is sick because he is not whole."

—Carl Gustav Jung

Notes

Mind-Body Connection

- Is the mind a function of the brain, a series of biochemical reactions, or is it a separate entity unto itself?
- This one question, perhaps more than any other, initiated the discipline of psychology.

Mind-Body Connection
(continued)

- In this chapter, we will look at how the mind perceives stress so that the "antiquated" stress response can be updated or re-circuited, highlighting some specific aspects of the psychology of stress.

Psychological Nature of Stress

- This chapter will review the nature of stress from a psychological view.
- Several theories will be explored, including the theories and views of:

- Sigmund Freud
- Carl Gustav Jung
- Elisabeth Kübler-Ross
- Viktor Frankl
- Wayne Dyer
- Leo Buscaglia
- Abraham Maslow
- A Tibetan perspective of mind

Sigmund Freud

- Freud believed that humans maintain a level of (instinctual) tension that arises from both internal sources (instinctual impulses) and external sources that attack our ego or identity.
- The ego copes with stress through the use of a host of defense mechanisms, including denial, repression, projection, rationalization, displacement, and humor.

Some of Freud's Defensive Mechanisms

- Denial (I didn't do it.)
- Repression (I don't remember doing it.)
- Projection (He did it.)
- Rationalization (Everyone does it.)
- Displacement (He made me do it.)
- Humor (I did it, and a year from now I'll laugh about it!)

Sigmund Freud
(continued)

- In Freud's opinion, there is a constant instinctual tension between body and mind as the mind attempts to cater to the biological and physiological impulses in socially acceptable ways.
- This internal tension can be decreased, but because of the power of human instincts, it is never fully extinguished.

Notes

Notes

_____
_____
_____
_____
_____
_____
_____
_____
_____
_____
_____
_____
_____
_____
_____
_____
_____
_____
_____
_____
_____
_____
_____
_____
_____
_____
_____
_____
_____
_____
_____
_____

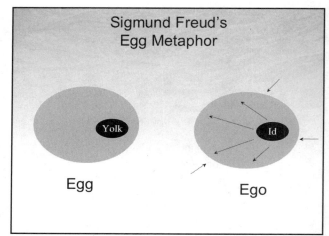

Sigmund Freud's Egg Metaphor

Yolk

Egg

Id

Ego

Carl Gustav Jung

- Proposed many theories of the mind and consciousness
- He coined many household words such as:
  - Introvert
  - Extrovert
  - Archetypes
  - Individuation
  - Synchronicity

Carl Gustav Jung
(continued)

- Jung theorized human personality as a process of self-discovery and realization, a concept he referred to as individuation
- Individuation involves not only the culmination of childhood experiences but a spiritual life force that shapes one's being and life direction

Carl Gustav Jung
(continued)

- Jung also suggested that there is a certain level of innate tension, psychic tension, which exists due to the language barrier between the conscious and unconscious minds.
- Individuation can reduce this tension through a continual soul searching that builds a bridge of understanding between the conscious and unconscious mind.

Elisabeth Kübler-Ross
(The death of unmet expectations)

- Kübler-Ross believed that stress can be aroused through the death of unmet expectations, which produces a series of mental processes.
- These processes are denial, anger, bargaining, depression, and acceptance
- Resolution of emotional baggage leads one to the final stage, acceptance which enhances inner peace.

Stages of Death and Grieving

1. Denial (This isn't happening)
2. Anger (I am furious this is happening)
3. Bargaining (Well, OK, as long as…)
4. Withdrawal (silence)
5. Acceptance (OK, this is it, now let's get on with things)

Never stated, yet implied, is the 6th stage:

6. Adaptation (How do I adapt to the situation?)

Notes

Viktor Frankl
(A search for the meaning of life)

- Frankl's psychological theories center around the concept of human pain and the meaning of suffering.
- Frankl believed that for life to be complete there must be suffering, but that there must also be a search for the meaning of the suffering to resolve the issues of emotional stress.

Viktor Frankl
(continued)

- Logotherapy
- Tragic optimism
- Noo-dynamics
- "Spirituality"

Wayne Dyer
(Guilt and worry)

- Dyer believes that guilt and worry are associated with virtually every stressor perceived by people in America.
- Guilt is an expression of self-anger; worry, a manifestation of fear.

Wayne Dyer
(continued)

- Guilt and worry immobilize the thought processes, distract one from the present moment, and thus make one unable to conquer stress and attain inner peace.

Wayne Dyer
(continued)

- Erroneous zones
  - Emotional zones that waste energy
- Left-over guilt
- Self-imposed guilt
- "The art of worrying"

Leo Buscaglia
(The lessons of self-love)

- Buscaglia believes that love is a response to a learned group of stimuli and behaviors; it is not innate, but taught.
- Buscaglia believes there are many degrees of love, from joy to grace, but there is only one love that leads to the positive growth process of self-discovery.

Notes

Leo Buscaglia
(continued)

- Chronic stress and low self-esteem
- Self-love and the X-factor
- Self-love and self-acceptance

Abraham Maslow
(The art of self-actualization)

- Maslow developed a humanistic approach to psychology that placed emphasis on personality traits, those reflections of inner resources that seem to help people cope with stress and achieve psychological health.
- Maslow's theory of motivation suggests that humans operate on a hierarchy of needs that influences behavior.

Maslow's Hierarchy of Needs

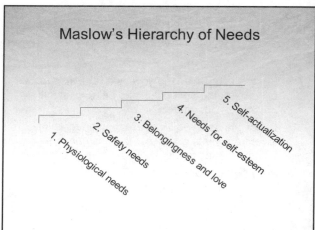

5. Self-actualization
4. Needs for self-esteem
3. Belongingness and love
2. Safety needs
1. Physiological needs

A Tibetan Perspective on the Mind and Stress

- The mind is comprised of the "self" (false self, ego driven self) and the "Self" (the true self or the aspect of the Higher Self).
- The goal is not to allow the "self" to overpower the "Self."
- Stress is a consequence of desires with attachments
- Let go of attachments and inner peace can be realized.

Study Guide Questions

1. According to Freud, what does the mind do to defend against stress?
2. According to Jung, what does the mind do (or could it do) to resolve stress?
3. According to Kübler-Ross, what process does the mind develop/use to cope with stress?
4. According to Frankl, this aspect needs to be addressed in coping successfully with stress.

Study Guide Questions
(continued)

5. According to Dyer, which two aspects perpetuate emotional stress?
6. According to Buscaglia, what is essential to cope/resolve personal issues of stress?
7. According to Maslow, which inner resources can be used to cope with stress?
8. What can be learned from the Tibetan culture about the mind and stress?
9. What are some common aspects to these theorists?

Notes

The Stress Emotions:
Anger and Fear

Chapter 5

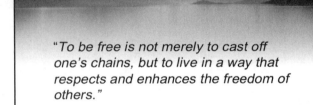

"*To be free is not merely to cast off one's chains, but to live in a way that respects and enhances the freedom of others.*"

—Nelson Mandela

Anger and Fear

• There are two emotions specifically associated with the stress response:
  – anger
  – fear
• Anger produces the urge to fight.
• Fear promotes the urge to run and hide.

Notes

The Anatomy of Anger

The Colors (Manifestations) of Anger

Impatience	Rage	Hostility
Prejudice	Sarcasm	Cynicism
Jealousy	Envy	Guilt
Frustration	Resentment	Fear

Others?

The Anatomy of Anger
(continued)

- Freud considered anger as the "Rage Reflex"
- Physiological responses to anger vs. fear
- Anger is an energizing emotion, fear is an energy-draining emotion
- Every anger episode is the result of unmet expectations
- The average person feels anger about 15–20 times per day

Gender Differences

- Both men and women feel anger the same way
- Culturally, men are allowed to express it (within reason)
- Culturally, women are not allowed to express it

Correcting the Myth of Catharsis

Not all venting of anger is good or healthy!

1. Cast anger in the right direction
2. Expression must offer a sense of self-control
3. Expression must not antagonize others
4. Expression of anger must be understood by others

Four Mismanaged Anger Styles

(Unresolved anger becomes a control issue)
- The Somatizer
- The Self-punisher
- The Exploder
- The Underhander
- All of these are inappropriate behaviors
- Everyone exhibits some of these behaviors, but typically one is more dominant in our personality
- Which is your most dominant mismanaged anger style?

The Somatizer

(Repressed anger manifested in the body)
- Temporomandibular joint disorder (TMJD)
- Migraines
- Rheumatoid arthritis
- Hypertension
- Liver problems
- Many women (but not all) tend to be somatizers

Notes

Notes

The Self-Punisher

(Guilt-produced obsessive behaviors)
- Excessive eating
- Excessive sleeping
- Excessive exercise
- Shopping
- Cutting (self-mutilation)

The Exploder

(Anger through intimidation)
- Road rage
- Phone rage
- Violent behavior (e.g., Columbine HS)
- Excessive swearing

The Underhander

(Passive-aggressive behavior)
- Sarcasm
- Late for meetings
- Not returning phone calls
- Padding one's expense account
- Seeking revenge

Creative Anger Strategies

- Know your anger style
- Learn to monitor your anger
- Learn to de-escalate your anger
- Learn to out-think your anger

Creative Anger Strategies
(continued)

- Get comfortable with all your feelings—express them constructively
- Plan ahead
- Develop a strong support system
- Develop realistic expectations of yourself and others

Creative Anger Strategies
(continued)

- Learn problem-solving techniques
- Stay in shape
- Turn complaints into requests
- Make past anger pass: forgiveness

Notes

Notes

_____
_____
_____
_____
_____
_____
_____
_____
_____
_____
_____
_____
_____
_____
_____
_____
_____
_____
_____
_____
_____
_____
_____
_____
_____
_____
_____
_____
_____
_____
_____
_____
_____

The Anatomy of Fear

The Colors (Manifestations) of Fear

Doubt	Anxiety
Suspicion	Agitation
Worry	Paranoia
Embarrassment	

Others?

The Anatomy of Fear (continued)

- Fear is a learned reaction
- Rational vs. irrational fears
- When is fear appropriate?
- When is fear unwarranted?

The Anatomy of Fear (Basic Human Fears)

- Fear of failure
- Fear of rejection
- Fear of the unknown
- Fear of death
- Fear of isolation
- Fear of the loss of self-dominance

Strategies to Overcome Fear

Fear must be confronted (diplomatically) to be resolved!

- Systematic desensitization (break fear into small manageable parts)
  (e.g., fear of flying classes by Lufthansa airlines)

- Fine tune expectations to meet the reality of the situation
- Learn to stop making excuses and stop beating yourself up
- Plan for the future, rather than worry about it—be proactive!

Depression: A By-Product of Anger/Fear

- High use of anti-depressants in America (33%)
- Depression—Anger turned inward?
- Symptoms:

  - Overwhelming sadness   - Perpetual blues
  - Prolonged grieving   - Feeling melancholy
  - Others _____

Depression: Antidepressants Only Treat Symptoms

"A chemical cure cannot heal emotional wounds."

—Susan Skog

Author, *Depression: What Your Body Is Trying to Tell You*

Notes

_____

_____

_____

_____

_____

_____

_____

_____

_____

_____

_____

_____

_____

_____

_____

_____

_____

_____

_____

_____

_____

_____

_____

_____

_____

_____

_____

_____

_____

_____

_____

_____

_____

_____

_____

_____

_____

_____

_____

_____

_____

_____

Study Guide Questions

1. Describe the emotion of anger (the fight response).
2. What ways is anger mismanaged? Name the four styles of mismanaged anger.
3. What are ways to help, cope, and manage unresolved anger feelings?
4. In what ways does fear manifest as stress?

Notes

Managing Stress
Principles and Strategies for Health and Well-Being

Stress-Prone and Stress-Resistant Personalities

Chapter 6

"When I was 25, I got testicular cancer and nearly died. I don't know why I am still alive. I can only guess. I have a tough constitution and my profession taught me how to compete against long odds and big obstacles."

—Lance Armstrong

Personality

- Personality is thought to comprise several:
  - traits
  - characteristics
  - behaviors
  - expressions
  - moods
  - feelings as perceived by others

Notes

Personality
(continued)

- The complexity of one's personality is thought to be shaped by:
  - genetic factors
  - family dynamics
  - social influences
  - personal experiences

Personality and Stress

- How we deal with stress is due in large part to our personalities, yet regardless of personality, we each exhibit many inner resources to use in the face of stress.
- New behaviors can be learned and adopted to aid in this coping process.
- We do not have to be passive victims to stress.

Stress-Prone Personalities

These personalities do not cope with stress well:
  - Type A personality
  - Codependent personality
  - Helpless-hopeless personality

Type A Behavior

- Time urgency
- Polyphasia (multitasking)
- Ultra-competitiveness
- Rapid speech patterns
- Manipulative control
- Hyperaggressiveness and free-floating hostility

Codependent Personality

- Ardent approval seekers
- Perfectionists
- Super-overachievers
- Crisis managers
- Devoted loyalists
- Self-sacrificing martyrs
- Manipulators
- "Victims"
- Feelings of inadequacy
- Reactionaries

Helpless-Hopeless Personality

- Poor self-motivation
- Cognitive distortion where perception of failure repeatedly eclipses prospects of success
- Emotional dysfunction
- External locus of control of reinforcing behavior

Notes

Stress-Resistant Personalities

These personalities cope with stress well:
1. Hardy Personality

2. Survivor Personality

3. Type R Personality (Sensation Seekers)

The Hardy Personality

- Based on the work of Maddi and Kobasa
- Three characteristics noted in those who cope well with stress:
  - Commitment (invests oneself in the solution)
  - Control (takes control of a situation, doesn't run from it)
  - Challenge (sees opportunity rather than the problems)

Survivor Personality Traits

- A person who responds rather than reacts to danger/stress
- Bi-phase traits (left and right brain skills)
  - Proud but humble
  - Selfish but altruistic
  - Rebellious but cooperative
  - Spiritual but irreverent
  - Considered optimists and good at creative problem solving

Type "R" Personality (Sensation Seekers)

- Zuckerman (1971) identified the sensation-seeking personality as those people who seek thrills and sensations but take calculated risks in their endeavors; they appear to be dominated by an adventurous spirit.

Self-Esteem: The Bottom-Line Defense

- Practices of high self-esteem:
  - Focus on action
  - Living consciously
  - Self-acceptance
  - Self-responsibility
  - Self-assertiveness
  - Living purposefully

Characteristics of High Self-Esteem

- Connectedness (support groups)
- Uniqueness (special qualities)
- Empowerment (uses inner resources)
- Role models or mentors (has others to look up to)
- Calculated risk taking (not motivated by fear)

Notes

1. List the stress-prone personalities and give an example of each.
2. List the stress-resistant personalities and give an example of each.
3. Describe self-esteem and what role this plays in promoting and resolving stress.

Notes

_____
_____
_____
_____
_____
_____
_____
_____
_____
_____
_____
_____
_____
_____
_____
_____
_____
_____
_____
_____
_____
_____
_____
_____
_____
_____
_____
_____
_____
_____
_____
_____
_____
_____
_____
_____
_____

Managing Stress
Principles and Strategies for Health and Well-Being

Stress and Human Spirituality

Chapter 7

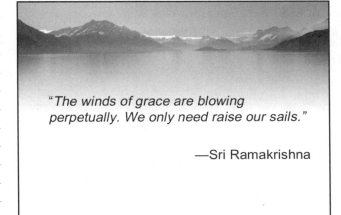

"The winds of grace are blowing perpetually. We only need raise our sails."

—Sri Ramakrishna

A Spiritual Hunger in Troubled Times

- Troubled times (personal and planetary) often promote a spiritual hunger
- People are seeking answers to questions posted in a troubled world
- We are living in troubled times
- Never before have people had access to the Ageless Wisdom as they have now (Internet, books, talk shows, etc.)

Notes

_____

_____

_____

_____

_____

_____

_____

_____

_____

_____

_____

_____

_____

_____

_____

_____

_____

_____

_____

_____

_____

_____

_____

_____

_____

_____

_____

_____

_____

_____

_____

_____

_____

_____

_____

_____

A Turning Point in Human Consciousness

Many things have contributed to a greater awareness of spirituality:
- *Apollo* Space Project (seeing the planet Earth as whole)
- Self-Help Groups (accessing one's high power)
- Popularity of Hebrew Kabalah (divine mysticism)
- Accounts of Near-Death Experiences
- Popularity of American Indian Spirituality
- Popularity of Oprah Winfrey show's message

Defining Human Spirituality

- The concept of spirituality is ineffable, it escapes the confines of human language. There are many words that come to mind when the term *spirituality* is mentioned:

-Higher consciousness	-Faith	-Transcendence
-Self-reliance	-Self-efficacy	-Mysticism
-Self-realization	-Self-actualization	-Community
-Enlightenment	-The Divine	-Love
-Others		

Defining Human Spirituality
(continued)

- Spirituality is not the same thing as religion
- Spirituality is inclusive, not exclusive
- Spirituality is experiential, not just theoretical
- Spirituality is knowing you are part of something much bigger than yourself
- Spirituality is the recognition of the Divine, whatever that means to you

Theories of Human Spirituality

- Spirituality is hard to verbalize, but metaphors work nicely
- Most every culture uses the metaphor of a mountain
- The mountaintop offers the best, clearest view of life
- They speak of the trek up a mountain as a spiritual path or journey
- Although there is only one destination, there are many paths to the top!

Theories of Human Spirituality
(continued)

- The Path of Carl Jung: Accessing your divine consciousness
- The Path of M. Scott Peck: Follow the road to spiritual growth
- The Path of Hildegard von Bingen: Life is a mystery to embrace
- The Path of Black Elk: Honor all aspects of Mother Earth
- The Path of Mathew Fox: Honor the aspects of creation spirituality

Theories of Human Spirituality
(continued)

- The Path of Joan Borysenko: Employ spiritual optimism
- The Path of Deepak Chopra: Honor the 7 spiritual laws of success
- The Path of Jesus: Practice unconditional love
- The Path of Joseph Campbell: Complete the hero's journey
- The Path of Lao Tzu: Seek balance and harmony in life
- The Path of Albert Einstein: All aspects of life are energy with a divine purpose

The Path of Carl Jung: Connecting with the Divine Consciousness

"As far as we can discern, the sole purpose of human existence is to kindle a light in the darkness of mere being."

—Carl G. Jung

Jung's View of the Mind

Conscious mind

Unconscious mind

Collective unconscious

The Path of M. Scott Peck: Four Stages of Spiritual Growth

"Love is part of the journey of the human spirit. Remember that when you get to the fourth stage, the Mystical Communal stage, you are really only at the beginning."

—M. Scott Peck

Peck's Stages of Human Spiritual Growth

Stage 1: Chaotic antisocial individual

Stage 2: Formal institutionalized individual

Stage 3: Skeptical individual

Stage 4: Mystic communal individual

**The Path of Hildegard von Bingen:
The Divine Mystery**

- Some things simply cannot be explained by science.
- It's best to simply appreciate the bigger mystery of life.

**The Path of Black Elk:
Mother Earth Spirituality**

"Every part of this earth is sacred to my people. We know the sap that runs through the trees as we know the blood that runs through our veins. We are part of the earth and it is part of us. Man did not weave the web of life, he is merely a strand in it. What he does to the earth he does to himself."
—Chief Seattle

Notes

Native American Medicine Wheel

Path of Introspection

Soul searching to find balance

Path of Quiet

Mental health through the lines of nature

Path of Peace

Youth and wonder

Path of Sun

Respectful of self, all people, and environment

The Path of Matthew Fox: Creation Spirituality

"I see the recovery of the ancient tradition of creation spirituality as a gift for our times. Perhaps ecology and cosmology can awaken our slumbering world and in doing so, awaken our slumbering spirits."

—Matthew Fox

The Path of Joan Borysenko: Spiritual Optimism

"Growth of the soul is our goal, and there are many ways to encourage that growth, such as through love, nature, healing our wounds, forgiveness, and service. The soul grows well when giving and receiving love."

—Joan Borysenko

The Path of Deepak Chopra: Seven Universal Laws

"Consciousness in motion expresses itself as the objects of the universe in the eternal dance of life. The physical laws of the universe are actually this whole process of divinity in motion, or consciousness in motion."

—Deepak Chopra

The Path of Jesus of Nazareth

- The power of unconditional love
- The power of forgiveness
- Honoring "The Golden Rule"

The Path of Joseph Campbell: The Hero's Journey

"We are at this moment participating in one of the very greatest leaps of the human spirit—to a knowledge not only of outside nature, but also our own deep inward mystery—the greatest leap ever."

—Joseph Campbell

Notes

Campbell's The Hero's Journey

- The Departure (into the unknown)
- Initiation(s) (confrontation of stressors)
- The Return Home (resolution, inner peace)

The Path of Lao Tzu: The Way of the Tao

"Why did the ancients cherish the Tao?
Because through it, we may find a world of peace,
leaving behind a world of cares, and hold the
greatest treasure under heaven."

—Lao Tzu

Four Principles of Taoism

- Principle of harmonious action
- Principle of oneness
- Principle of cyclical growth
- Principle of dynamic balance

The Path of Albert Einstein

"God does not play dice with the Universe."

—Albert Einstein

Common Themes of Spirituality

- (Also known as "Seasons of the Soul")
  - Centering (Autumn)
  - Emptying (Winter)
  - Grounding (Spring)
  - Connecting (Summer)
- We go through many seasons in one lifetime
- We can go through many seasons at once with several life events

The Centering Process

- Taking time to go inside and do some soul searching

The Emptying Process

- Letting go of thoughts and perceptions (stress) that hold you back
- The hardest season to weather: very stressful for some to let go
- Emptying is entering the abyss, the void in which to cleanse and release
- This season is often called the "dark night of the soul"; it's also called "the winter of discontent"
- People often get stuck in this season due to grief, stress, depression

The Grounding Process

- A time to process and reflect on new insights to guide you
- Exhilaration often comes when new insights arrive. Eureka!

The Connecting Process

- A time to share what insights you have learned with others (Greed is not a spiritual value)
- This season is the "Disney World" experience of spirituality

A Model of Spirituality

Wisdom keepers cite four aspects of human spirituality:

1. Relationships
   -An insightful internal relationship
   -Powerful external (interpersonal) relationships
2. Values (personal value system)
3. A meaningful purpose in life
4. Appreciating the divine mystery of life

A Model of Spirituality
(continued)

- Spiritual potential (the potential of one's inner resources)
- Spiritual health (the utilization of one's inner resources)
- Roadblocks on the spiritual path (everyday stressors)
- Distractions on the spiritual path (attractions that become distractions)
- Interventions to promote spiritual health (nearly every stress management skill)

Importance of Spiritual Well-Being

- Ageless wisdom conveys that spiritual well-being is the cornerstone to wellness
- Stress and spirituality are inseparable partners in the dance of life
- Stress is now defined as the feeling of separation from one's divine source
- As global stress increases, there is a greater need to reestablish this connection

Notes

_____

Current Research on Spirituality and Health

- Health status and church attendance
- Healing power of prayer

- *Note:* Because spirituality is hard to define and difficult/impossible to measure, researchers have opted to measure aspects of religiosity, thus adding to the confusion of spirituality and religion.

Study Guide Questions

1. Define human spirituality (as best you can).
2. Select four theories of human spirituality and explain each (e.g., Jung, Peck, Black Elk, Jesus of Nazareth, Borysenko, Campbell, Lao Tzu, etc.).
3. Define and explain the common bonds of human spirituality (centering, emptying, grounding, and connecting processes).

Study Guide Questions
(continued)

4. Explain how relationships, values, and a meaningful purpose in life are affected by stress.
5. Define the concepts spiritual potential and spiritual health.
6. Define the concepts of spiritual roadblocks and distractions in terms of spiritual health.

Notes

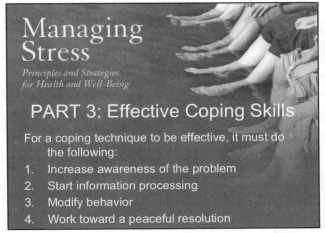

Managing Stress
Principles and Strategies for Health and Well-Being

PART 3: Effective Coping Skills

For a coping technique to be effective, it must do the following:

1. Increase awareness of the problem
2. Start information processing
3. Modify behavior
4. Work toward a peaceful resolution

Managing Stress
Principles and Strategies for Health and Well-Being

Cognitive Restructuring

Chapter 8

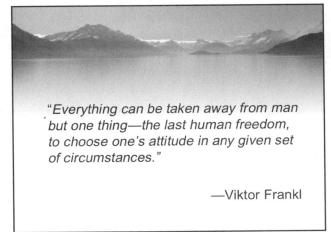

"Everything can be taken away from man but one thing—the last human freedom, to choose one's attitude in any given set of circumstances."

—Viktor Frankl

Perception and Interpretation

- All stimuli received by the brain are processed through interpretation and classified as negative, neutral, or positive; this process is called perception.

Albert Ellis

- The premise of Ellis's work was that stress-related behaviors are initiated by perceptions and that these self-defeating perceptions can be changed.

Cognitive Restructuring

- Cognitive restructuring means changing a perception from a negative interpretation to a neutral or positive one, making it less stressful.
- This process is also called reappraisal, relabeling, reframing, and attitude adjustment.

The Information-Processing Model

- Sensory input
- Sensory manipulation
- Cognitive/behavioral output
- Feedback system

Toxic Thoughts

- Negative thoughts are often called toxic thoughts.
- Research has now substantiated the hypothesis that negative thoughts can suppress the immune system.
- Borysenko calls creating negative thoughts awfulizing, and explains that the way to change these thoughts is through reframing.

Optimism and Luck
(An Attitude)

- Maximize your opportunities
- Listen to your intuition
- Focus on the positive
- Find the good in every bad situation

Notes

_____

_____

_____

_____

_____

_____

_____

_____

_____

_____

_____

_____

_____

_____

_____

_____

_____

_____

_____

_____

_____

_____

_____

_____

_____

_____

_____

_____

_____

_____

_____

_____

_____

_____

_____

_____

_____

_____

_____

A Four-Stage Process for Cognitive Restructuring

- Awareness
- Reappraisal of the situation
- Adoption and substitution
- Evaluation

Additional Tips for Cognitive Restructuring

- Initiate a relaxation technique to calm your mind
- Take responsibility for your own thoughts
- Fine-tune your expectations
- Give yourself positive affirmations
- Accentuate the positive

Examples of Positive Affirmation Statements

- "I am calm and relaxed."

- "I am healthy and whole."

- "I am a loveable person."

- "I am a college graduate."

Best Application of Cognitive Restructuring

- Use this technique when you find yourself continually whining
- Use positive affirmations to boost self-esteem throughout the day
- Use positive affirmations during stressful times (e.g., traffic, exams, etc.)

Study Guide Questions

1. What is the thinking process model?

2. How can you best describe toxic thoughts?

3. List the steps to initiate cognitive restructuring (reframing).

Notes

Notes

Managing Stress
*Principles and Strategies
for Health and Well-Being*

Behavior Modification

Chapter 9

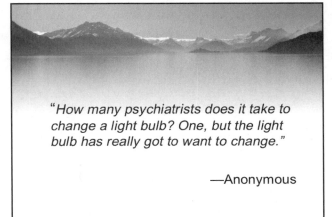

"*How many psychiatrists does it take to change a light bulb? One, but the light bulb has really got to want to change.*"

—Anonymous

Behavior as a Component of Personality

- Personality is thought to be comprised of:
  - values, those abstract qualities that give meaning to our lives
  - attitudes, perceptions derived from these values
  - behaviors, any actions based on one or more attitudes
- Of these, behaviors are thought to be the most easily influenced.

Notes

Some Theories of Human Behavior

- Classical Conditioning
  - based on Pavlov's dog research
  - e.g., smelling cookies makes you hungry
- Operant Conditioning
  - based on B. F. Skinner's work
  - e.g., rewards and punishment
- Modeling
  - copying others' behavior
  - e.g., Brad Pitt and Cameron Diaz bleach their hair and you do too!

The Behavior Modification Model

- Awareness
- Desire to change
- Cognitive restructuring
- Behavioral substitution
- Evaluation

Assertiveness Skills

- Learn to say no and not feel guilty
- Learn to use "I" statements
- Use eye contact
- Use assertive body language
- Practice peaceful disagreement
- Avoid manipulation
- Respond rather than react

Steps to Initiate Behavior Modification

- Select an undesirable behavior
- Ask yourself how motivated you are to change this behavior
- Think about what changes in your perceptions and attitudes must accompany this behavioral change
- Specify what new behavior you wish to adopt
- Evaluate

Best Application of Behavior Modification

- If you find you have a stress-prone behavior and wish to change it, follow the steps for behavior modification.

Study Guide Questions

1. Explain the difference between values, attitudes, and beliefs.
2. List and explain three different behavior models.
3. Explain the behavior modification model.
4. Explain the concept of assertiveness and list three assertiveness skills.

Notes

Notes

Managing Stress
Principles and Strategies for Health and Well-Being

Journal Writing

Chapter 10

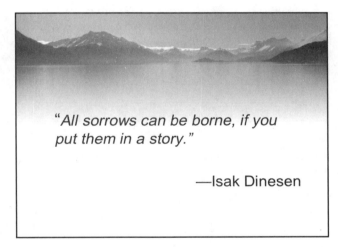

"All sorrows can be borne, if you put them in a story."

—Isak Dinesen

Historical Perspective of Journal Writing

- For centuries, people have chronicled their personal thoughts
- Early explorers kept journals of their explorations

Notes

_____
_____
_____
_____
_____
_____
_____
_____
_____
_____
_____
_____
_____
_____

Journal Writing

- Journal writing can be defined as a series of written passages that document the personal events, thoughts, feelings, memories, and perceptions in one's journey throughout life leading to wholeness.
- The practice of journal writing has proven a formidable coping technique to deal with stress.

Journal Writing
(continued)

Journal writing is said to promote emotional catharsis when thoughts, perceptions, attitudes, values, beliefs, and the tensions these create are allowed to work themselves out on paper.

Journal Writing as a Coping Technique

- Short-term benefits include releasing pent-up feelings of anger and anxiety.
- Long-term benefits include seeing patterns and habits of thought, perceptions, and behaviors that are not detectable on an entry-to-entry basis.

Notes

Steps to Initiate Effective Journal Writing

- Essential elements for effective journal writing include:
  - a journal notebook
  - a pen or pencil
  - a quiet place to write uninterrupted
  - an open and honest mind

Additional Suggestions for Journal Writing

- Try to identify those concerns, problems, and issues that cause the most frustration, grief, and tension.
- Ask yourself what emotions are elicited when these stressors are encountered.
- Allow the writing process to augment your creative processes to further resolution.

Of Blogs and Journals

- Blogs may offer a means of self-expression (and catharsis) through writing, but blogs are not the same as journal writing.
- Journals are confidential.
- Blogs are public opinions expressed to the world.

Notes

_____

_____

_____

_____

_____

_____

_____

_____

_____

_____

_____

_____

_____

_____

_____

_____

_____

_____

_____

_____

_____

_____

_____

_____

_____

_____

_____

_____

_____

_____

_____

_____

_____

_____

_____

_____

Best Application of Journal Writing

- A great way to release pent-up feelings
- A great way to start resolving issues

Study Guide Questions

1. Explain how journaling is used as an effective coping technique.
2. Differentiate between the immediate effects and long-term effects of journal writing.
3. List several steps that help promote the journal writing process.

Notes

_____

_____

_____

_____

_____

_____

_____

_____

_____

_____

_____

_____

_____

_____

_____

_____

_____

_____

_____

_____

_____

_____

_____

_____

_____

_____

_____

_____

_____

_____

_____

_____

_____

_____

_____

_____

_____

_____

_____

_____

"Draw me how you feel."

—Sharlene Gin

The Origins of Art Therapy

- Art as a personal expression dates back to prehistoric times.
- Art as a form of psychotherapy dates back to Freud and Jung.
- In 1969 the American Art Therapy Association was founded.

Notes

What Is Art Therapy?

- Art therapy is described as the creative use of art to provide for nonverbal expression and communication through which to foster self-awareness and personal growth.

Goals of Art Therapy

- Art therapy is recognized for its many therapeutic effects on aspects of mental, physical, spiritual, and most notably, emotional well-being.

Goals of Art Therapy
(continued)

- To provide a means for strengthening the ego
- To provide a cathartic experience
- To provide a means to uncover anger
- To offer an avenue to reduce guilt
- To facilitate impulse control
- To help patients/clients use as a new outlet during incapacitating illness

Clinical Uses of Art Therapy

- Veteran hospitals
- Eating disorders
- Criminals
- Abused children
- Drug rehabilitation
- Emotionally disturbed
- Young children
- College students
- Cancer patients
- Chronic pain

Steps to Initiate Art Therapy

- Getting past artist roadblocks
- A choice of materials
- Illustrative themes
- Interpretations

Interpretations

- Every line, point, color, and image means something
- Interpretations may not be immediate to the artist
- Only the artist is best qualified to make an interpretation
- The role of a therapist is to aid the artist in this process
- Interpretations are part of the healing process

Notes

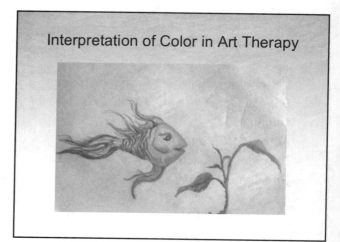

Interpretation of Color in Art Therapy

Illustrative Themes

- Draw yourself
- Draw something that represents you
- Draw a fantasy animal
- Close your eyes and draw a line on paper
- Draw a house
- Draw an expression of anger/fear
- Draw a healing image of you
- Draw a peaceful image
- Draw how you feel right now
- Draw a dream image

Best Application of Art Therapy

- A great way to call on the wisdom of the unconscious mind
- A great way to release emotions that are pent up
- A great way to start the resolution process of a stressor

Study Guide Questions

1. Explain how art therapy is used as an effective coping technique.
2. What archetypal meaning do the colors represent or symbolize in art therapy?
3. List several steps (themes) that help promote art therapy as a coping technique.

Notes

Notes

Managing Stress
Principles and Strategies for Health and Well-Being

Humor Therapy
(Comic Relief)

Chapter 12

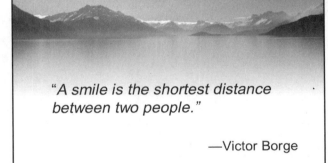

"A smile is the shortest distance between two people."

—Victor Borge

An Historical Perspective of Humor Therapy

- Oldest records of comic relief date back to ancient Greece
- Bible passage in proverbs is often cited as well
  - "A merry heart does good like medicine."
- Medieval kings and queens had court jesters
- In the Victorian age laughing was thought to be sinful
- The roaring '20s seemed to have changed all that

Notes

_____
_____
_____
_____
_____
_____
_____
_____
_____
_____
_____
_____
_____
_____
_____
_____
_____
_____
_____
_____
_____
_____
_____
_____
_____
_____
_____
_____
_____
_____
_____
_____

Norman Cousins and Humor Therapy

- Anatomy of an illness
- Is there a correlation between stress—particularly negative perceptions and emotions—and disease?
- The premise of humor therapy is that if negative thoughts can result in illness and disease, positive thoughts should enhance health

Types of Humor

- Parody
- Satire
- Slapstick comedy
- Absurd/nonsense
- Double entendre
- Black humor
- Irony
- Sarcasm
- Dry humor, quick wit and puns
- Bathroom humor

Types of Senses of Humor

- Conventional Humor
- Life of the Party Humor
- Creative Sense of Humor
- Good Sport Sense of Humor

Theories of Humor

Reasons why we laugh and smile
- Superiority Theory (Plato): Emotionally based
- Release/Relief Theory (Freud): Physically based
- Incongruity Theory: Mentally based
- Divinity Theory: Spiritually based

Psychology of Humor

- Humor is a wonderful defense mechanism
- Humor helps diffuse anger and fear
- Humor can also serve as a distraction from stress
- Only sarcasm is considered negative (it produces stress)
- Humor is used in many settings, from hospitals to recovery programs

Physiology of Humor

- Relaxes muscles
- Reduces blood pressure
- Increases ventilation
- Massages internal organs
- Promotes secretion of neuropeptides

Notes

Notes

_____

Physiology of Humor
(continued)

- Research investigating the psycho-neuroimmunological effects of laughter have found that there is a strong relationship between good health and good humor. In essence, laughter helps restore physiological homeostasis.

Steps to Initiate Humor Therapy

- Learn not to take yourself too seriously.
- Find one humorous thing a day.
- Work to improve your imagination and creativity.
- Start a joke/cartoon of the week swap with a friend.
- Learn to hyperexaggerate when telling a story.

Steps to Initiate Humor Therapy
(continued)

- Build a humor library.
- Build a tickler notebook.
- Find a host of varied humor venues.
- Access your humor network.
- Improve your self-esteem daily.

Best Application of Comic Relief

- Humor is a great way to relieve stress
- Humor serves to balance one's emotions
- Best to achieve the quota of 15 laughs per day
- List some additional ways you can hit this quota

Study Guide Questions

1. How is humor best defined?

2. List five different types of humor.

3. List and explain the four theories of humor (why we smile and laugh).

Study Guide Questions
(continued)

4. Each humor theory can be associated with one of the wellness paradigm components. Which goes with which?

5. How does humor and laughter work as a coping technique for stress?

6. List four ways to incorporate more humor/laughter into your life.

Notes

Notes

Managing Stress
Principles and Strategies for Health and Well-Being

Creative Problem Solving

Chapter 13

"*Make it a practice to keep on the lookout for novel and interesting ideas that others have used successfully. Your idea only has to be original in its adaptation to the problem you are working on.*"

—Thomas Alva Edison

The Importance of Creative Problem Solving

- We live in a world where there appear to be more problems than solutions, making life potentially stressful.
- Every problem has more than one solution, but to waste creative efforts only leads to more stress
- Employing your creative skills is empowering.
- It's always good to brush up on your creative skills.

Notes

The Creative Process Described by Maslow

- Maslow called the creative process the "art of being happily lost in the present moment."
- Maslow divided the creative process into:
  - primary creativity (origin of ideas)
  - secondary creativity (strategic plan)

Roger von Oech's Four Phases of Creative Thinking

- The Explorer—looks for ideas
- The Artist— plays with ideas
- The Judge—judges and selects the best ideas
- The Warrior—champions the best idea

The Biggest Danger in the Creative Process

The biggest problem in the creative process is getting the order wrong. The judge goes third, not first, but most people forget this and let the judge go first, thus squelching every potential idea. This is creative suicide!

"If your only tool is a hammer, you'll see every problem as a nail."

—Abraham Maslow

Connect all 9 dots with 4 straight lines. Go through each dot only once. Do not lift your pencil from the paper.

Obstacles to the Creative Process

- "The right answer."
- "I'm not creative."
- "Don't be foolish."
- "To err is wrong."

Notes

_____
_____
_____
_____
_____
_____
_____
_____
_____
_____
_____
_____
_____
_____
_____
_____
_____
_____
_____
_____
_____
_____
_____
_____
_____
_____
_____
_____
_____
_____
_____
_____
_____
_____
_____
_____
_____
_____
_____
_____
_____
_____

Arthur VanGundy's Obstacles to the Creative Process

- Perceptual roadblocks
- Emotional roadblocks
- Intellectual roadblocks
- Cultural roadblocks
- Environmental roadblocks

A Creative Problem-Solving Strategy

- Describe the problem or issue.
- Generate some viable ideas.
- Select the best idea(s) and refine.
- Implement the best idea.
- Evaluate the outcome. (Did it work? Why or why not? If not, start over again to find the best solution.)

The Map of Creative Problem Solving

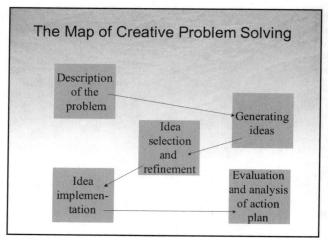

Best Application of Creative Problem Solving

- We are all bound to have problems to solve from small issues to huge dilemmas.
- We all have the skills (four aspects of creativity) to use in every situation.
- Creative problem solving will prove to be your most valuable coping skill for every stressor.

Study Guide Questions

1. Why is creativity thought to be such an important coping technique?

2. Describe the four stages of von Oech's creative thinking process model.

3. Why is the order so important in this model?

Study Guide Questions
(continued)

4. What are four common "blocks" to the creative process?

5. List the five steps in the creative problem-solving process.

Notes

Notes

Managing
Stress
*Principles and Strategies
for Health and Well-Being*

Communication Skills

Chapter 14

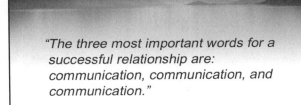

"The three most important words for a successful relationship are: communication, communication, and communication."

—Anonymous

Verbal Communication

- Verbal language is a series of expressive thoughts and perceptions described through word symbols.
- Linguistic experts divide verbal communication into two components:
  - encoding
  - decoding

Verbal Communication
(continued)

- Encoding is the process wherein a speaker attempts to frame thoughts and perceptions into words (e.g., someone saying to the person next to her, "Boy, it's stuffy in here").

Verbal Communication
(continued)

- Decoding is the process wherein the message is translated, dissected, analyzed, and interpreted by the listener (e.g., the person hearing this thinks, "Yeah, the room does smell rather gamy").
- During the encoding and decoding process, some thoughts can get lost in translation.
- Misunderstanding, confusion, and stress can arise anywhere in this process.

Communication Styles Between Genders

"Men may be from Mars and women may be from Venus, but right now both sexes are living on earth so we better learn to speak the same language."

—Lily Tomlin

Nonverbal Communication

- Nonverbal communication is described as any communication that does not involve words. It may include:
  - postures
  - facial expressions
  - touch
  - even style of clothing

Nonverbal Communication
(continued)

- Nonverbal communication differs from verbal communication in that it is multichanneled—addressing all senses—not merely stimuli received through the sense of hearing.
- Nonverbal communication is not only indirect, but often unconscious.

Listening, Attending, and Responding Skills

- Assume the role of listener
- Maintain eye contact.
- Avoid word prejudice.
- Use "minimal encouragers."
- Paraphrase what was said to ensure understanding.

Notes

Listening, Attending, and Responding Skills (continued)

- Ask questions to improve clarity of statements.
- Use empathy to reflect and share feelings.
- Provide feedback.
- Summarize the content of what was said.

Conflict Resolution and Management Styles

- Conflict Resolution
  - Content conflict
  - Values conflict
  - Ego conflict
- Management Style
  - Withdrawal (-)
  - Surrender (-)
  - Hostile aggression (-)
  - Persuasion (-/+)
  - Dialogue (+)

Steps to Enhance Communication Skills

- Speak with precision and directness.
- Enhance your vocabulary.
- Use appropriate language for listening.
- Attack issues, not people.
- Avoid making people defensive.

Notes

Steps to Enhance Communication Skills
(continued)

- Talk to people yourself, not through others.
- Avoid information overload.
- Validate your assumptions.
- Resolve problems when they arise.

Best Application of Communication Skills

- For every stressor that involves another person, communication skills are essential to resolve the issue at hand.
- If nothing else, remember this: Attack issues, not people.
- Be a good diplomat!

Study Guide Questions

1. Why do many stress-related problems involve poor communications?

2. List three aspects of good verbal communication.

3. List three aspects of nonverbal communication.

4. List the five conflict management styles and highlight the most effective one.

5. What are five ways to improve your communication style?

Notes

Managing Stress
Principles and Strategies
for Health and Well-Being

Resource Management:
Managing Time and Money

Chapter 15

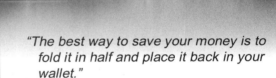

"The best way to save your money is to fold it in half and place it back in your wallet."

— Anonymous

Money Management

Time and money (the lack of) are often listed as people's top stressors.

Americans tend to spend money they don't have (massive credit card debt).

Americans tend to have little or no savings.
The combined effect can spell financial ruin.

Notes

_____
_____
_____
_____
_____
_____
_____
_____
_____
_____
_____
_____
_____
_____
_____
_____
_____
_____
_____
_____
_____
_____
_____
_____
_____
_____
_____
_____
_____
_____
_____
_____
_____
_____
_____
_____
_____
_____
_____
_____
_____

Money Management (continued)

Money Matters:
Simple rules of financial management
1. Make a personal budget and follow it.
2. Don't spend what you don't have.
3. Pay all of your bills on time.
4. Save 10% of your monthly earnings.

Money Management (continued)

Money Matters:

Good financial management means avoiding the mass marketing appeals to your ego to buy, buy, and buy!

Money Management (continued)

Tips for Achieving Financial Freedom

1. Make and follow an honest budget.
2. Live a sustainable lifestyle.
3. Freeze your credit cards.
4. Keep a spending journal.
5. See each purchase as an investment
6. Consolidate your debt.

Money Management
(continued)

More Tips for Financial Freedom

7. Remove yourself from the temptation to buy.
8. Ask "why" before you buy.
9. Don't buy on impulse...wait a day or two.
10. Be wary of bargains.
11. Clean your house!
12. Learn to say no when you're out with friends.

Time Is a Man-Made Concept

We have become slaves to, rather than masters of, time.

Time Management

Time-management skills are now taught to people, from grade school to corporate America, to help them gain a sense of control over personal responsibilities.

Notes

_____

Time Management
(continued)

Multi-tasking (e.g., eating, talking on the cell phone, and driving to work or school) is not an effective means to managing your time.

Time Management Defined!

- Time management is the ability to prioritize, schedule, and execute personal responsibilities to personal satisfaction.

Personality Styles and Behavior

- The Type A person
- The workaholic
- The time juggler
- The procrastinator
- The perfectionist
- Lifestyle behavior trap

Notes

Steps to Initiate Time-Management Techniques

- Prioritization
  - ABC rank order method
  - Pareto principle
  - Important vs. urgent method

Steps to Initiate Time-Management Techniques (continued)

- Scheduling
  - Boxing
  - Time mapping (short blocks of time)
  - Clustering (group responsibilities)

Steps to Initiate Time-Management Techniques (continued)

- Execution
  - Assign specific deadlines
  - Break large projects into small tasks
  - Work on one section or task at a time
  - Reward your accomplishments

Notes

Additional Time-Management Ideas

- Learn to delegate responsibilities
- Schedule personal time each day.
- Learn to schedule interruptions.
- Carry and use an idea book.

Additional Time-Management Ideas
(continued)

- Edit your life.
- Refine your organization skills.
- Refine your networking skills.
- Bring balance back into your life.

Best Application of Time Management

- Be sure to include flexibility in your time management plan.
- Be sure to include other stress management techniques as well.

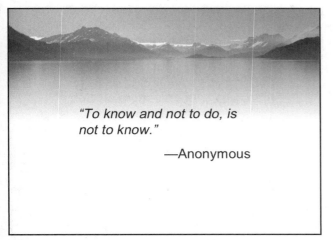

"To know and not to do, is not to know."

—Anonymous

Study Guide Questions

1. List the four rules for financial stability.

2. Describe the psychology of money.

3. List five tips to help achieve financial freedom.

Study Guide Questions
(continued)

4. Explain the following time-management concepts:
- Pareto principle
- Boxing
- Time mapping
- Clustering

Notes

_____
_____
_____
_____
_____
_____
_____
_____
_____
_____
_____
_____
_____
_____
_____
_____
_____
_____
_____
_____
_____
_____
_____
_____
_____
_____
_____
_____
_____
_____
_____
_____
_____
_____
_____
_____
_____
_____
_____

Study Guide Questions
(continued)

5. List five effective strategies to help managing your time more efficiently:
   1.
   2.
   3.
   4.
   5.

Notes

Managing Stress
Principles and Strategies for Health and Well-Being

Additional Coping Techniques

Chapter 16

"One cannot collect all the beautiful shells on the beach, one can collect only a few."

—Anne Morrow Lindbergh

A Wealth of Coping Techniques

- There are hundreds of ways to cope with stress
- Coping techniques that work toward a resolution are deemed effective
- Coping techniques that don't work are deemed ineffective

Notes

Ineffective Coping Strategies

- All coping techniques that avoid stress rather than confront it are ineffective
- Our worst health concerns are examples of poor coping techniques
- Drinking that leads to alcoholism
- Fighting that leads to spousal abuse
- Drug experimentation that leads to addiction
- Avoidance of any kind that perpetuates stress

Essential Aspects of Effective Coping Skills

1. Increase your awareness of the cause of stress
2. Process information about your stressors
3. Change attitude, change behavior
4. Work toward a peaceful resolution

Information Seeking

- Lack of information and fear of the unknown can lead to stress
- To conquer fear of the unknown, gather information about a specific circumstance
- Collecting and processing facts can solve the problem and regain emotional stability

Social Engineering

- Define your stressor
- Identify your initial response
- Generate alternatives
- Choose the best alternative
- Evaluate the outcome of your choice

Additional Coping Techniques

- Social support groups
- Hobbies
- Forgiveness
- Dream therapy
- Prayer

Social Support Groups

- Friends, family are essential to help buffer the effects of crisis
- Support groups enhance feelings of acceptance
- Research supports the impact of support groups
  - classic breast cancer support group study

Notes

Hobbies

- Hobbies serve as a good mental escape
- Hobbies help make order out of chaos (gardening)
- Organizational skills can transfer to other aspects of life
- Cautionary note: Hobbies can produce stress at times

Forgiveness

- Forgiveness is considered an antidote for anger
- Forgiveness is done for you, not the person who wronged you
- Forgiveness is a means of letting go so you can move on with your life
- Forgiveness doesn't mean restitution, don't wait for an apology
- Forgiveness also involves the aspect of acceptance

Dream Therapy

- Freud called dreams the royal road to the unconscious
- Freud said dreams conceal the truth
- Jung said dreams reveal the truth
- Dreams can offer insight to resolve personal issues

Prayer and Faith

- Prayer is considered to be one of the oldest coping techniques
- Prayer is one of the top coping skills for older adults
- There are several different methods of prayers
- Prayer: building a bond with a higher power
- Prayer is not the same thing as meditation

Ways to Pray

(Note a similar style to visualization technique)

1. Send a clear transmission
2. Communicate in the present tense
3. Express your thoughts in a positive mind frame

Best Aspects of Employing Effective Coping Skills

- Unresolved stress can be devastating. These coping skills help to resolve issues so you can get on with your life.

Notes

_____

_____

_____

_____

_____

_____

_____

_____

_____

_____

_____

_____

_____

_____

_____

_____

_____

_____

_____

_____

_____

_____

_____

_____

_____

_____

_____

_____

_____

_____

_____

_____

_____

_____

_____

_____

_____

_____

Study Guide Questions
1. How does information seeking both reduce and promote stress?
2. Why are support groups thought to serve as an effective coping skill?
3. How do hobbies help one to reduce stress?

Study Guide Questions (continued)
4. Why is forgiveness considered an effective coping skill?
5. How can dream therapy help one reduce stress?
6. Why is prayer considered an effective coping technique?

Notes

Managing Stress
Principles and Strategies
for Health and Well-Being

Part 4: Relaxation Techniques

Effective Relaxation Techniques

Purpose of Relaxation Techniques:
- To return to homeostasis
- To reverse the effects of the stress response
- To engage the parasympathetic NS
- To alleviate the symptoms of stress

Effective Relaxation Techniques
(continued)

Every relaxation technique engages one or more of the five senses:

- Sight (e.g., visualization)
- Sound (e.g., music therapy)
- Taste (e.g., comfort foods)
- Smell (e.g., aromatherapy)
- Touch (e.g., muscle massage)

Effective Relaxation Techniques
(continued)

- There are hundreds of ways to relax
- Sleep is not the same thing as relaxation
  - (high blood pressure and muscle tension can occur during dreams)

Mind-Body Connection

Although the relaxation techniques are geared to reduce the symptoms of stress (e.g., blood pressure, heart rate, muscle tension) the mind and body cannot be separated and the mind benefits as well.

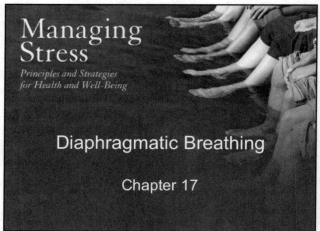

Managing Stress
Principles and Strategies for Health and Well-Being

Diaphragmatic Breathing

Chapter 17

"Let the air breathe for you."

—Emmett Miller, M.D.

Diaphragmatic Breathing

- Is one of the easiest and most effective methods of relaxation
- It is controlled, deep breathing
- In the practice of yoga, this technique is called the *pranayama*

Thoracic Breathing and the Stress Response

- By and large, Americans are thoracic breathers
- We breathe with the emphasis on our upper chest
- The consequences include slight pressure on the sternum and pressure on the solar plexus nerve.
- This tends to trigger a slight stress response causing:
  - A rise in heart rate, blood pressure, and other parameters
- Thoracic breathing does not promote relaxation
- Everyone employs belly breathing when they sleep!

Notes

The Mystery of the Breath

- Breath is considered by many to be the universal life force of energy
  - (e.g., chi, pranayama, etc.)
- Breath is synonymous with the word "spirit" in many cultures
- We infer spirit with the word breath with the words:
  - Inspiration
  - Expiration

Steps to Initiate Diaphragmatic Breathing

- Assume a comfortable position

- Concentration

- Visualization

Four Phases of Concentrated Diaphragmatic Breathing

- Phase I: Inspiration (Long)
- Phase II: A very slight pause before exhaling (Short)
- Phase III: Exhalation (Long)
- Phase IV: Another slight pause after exhalation before the next inhalation is initiated (Short)

Other Techniques and Diaphragmatic Breathing

- The majority of effective relaxation techniques integrate belly breathing

-Hatha Yoga

-T'ai Chi

-PMR

-Autogentic Training

-Others

-Massage Therapy

-Music Therapy

-Biofeedback

-Visualization

Diaphragmatic Breathing and Chronic Pain

- Breathing is often used to help people with chronic pain, both as a means to lessen the pain and serve as a pleasant distraction from pain.
- It's no secret that breathing is used for acute pain, as with Lamaze breathing during childbirth.

Visualization and Diaphragmatic Breathing

- Visualization exercise I: Breathing clouds
- Visualization exercise II: Alternate nostril breathing
- Visualization exercise III: Energy breathing

Notes

_____
_____
_____
_____
_____
_____
_____
_____
_____
_____
_____
_____
_____
_____
_____
_____
_____
_____
_____
_____
_____
_____
_____
_____
_____
_____
_____
_____
_____
_____
_____
_____
_____
_____
_____
_____
_____
_____

Best Application of Diaphragmatic Breathing

- This technique can be done anywhere (e.g., driving, exams, falling asleep, etc.)
- This technique can be done relatively shortly for an effect (5-10 minutes)
- Never underestimate the power of a good sigh!

Study Guide Questions

1. What is diaphragmatic breathing and why is this thought to be more relaxing than thoracic breathing?

2. Name the four phases of the breath cycle.

3. What three steps are important to engage in diaphragmatic breathing?

Study Guide Questions
(continued)

4. List four places you can do this relaxation technique.

5. List three other relaxation techniques that also include diaphragmatic breathing.

Notes

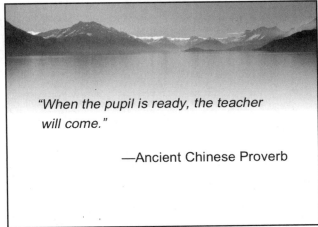

Notes

An Historical Perspective of Meditation

- Roots of meditation date back to Asia
- Every culture around the globe practices some form of meditation as a means to quiet the mind and gain clarity of thought
- Meditation is now synonymous with the term *centering*
- Meditation—it's not what you think!

Living in the Age of Information Overload

- Too much sensory stimulation tires the mind.
- A tired mind is a stressed mind, the consequences can lead to everything from poor communications to car accidents.
- Today over 25 million Americans meditate regularly.
- Metaphorically speaking, meditation is like emptying your unwanted emails to make more room for new information.

Meditation

- When the mind is emptied of superfluous conscious thoughts and ego chatter, insights can bubble up from the unconscious mind. This is what mystics refer to as "receiving enlightenment." This explains the Chinese proverb:

"When the student is ready, the teacher will come."

Types of Meditation

- **Exclusive Meditation** (focusing on only one thought, to the exclusion of all others—also called restrictive meditation)
- **Inclusive Meditation** (allowing all thoughts to enter the mind's screen, yet passing no judgment or emotional attachment on them)
- **Mindfulness Meditation** (being mindful/conscious of everything you do without judgment; some people consider this to be a form of inclusive meditation)

Vehicles for Exclusive Meditation

- Mental repetition (mantra)
- Visual concentration (tratek)
- Repeated sounds (nadem)
- Physical repetition (breathing, rhythmic exercise)
- Tactile repetition (beads, shell, stone, etc.)

Examples of Exclusive Meditation

- Transcendental Meditation (TM)
- The Relaxation Response

Inclusive Meditation

- Observance with emotional detachment
- Examples include:
  - Zen meditation
  - Mindfulness mediation

Zen Meditation

- Purpose of life
- *Koan*
- One with the universe
- Contemplative thought

- Divine enlightenment

Split-Brain Theory

- Left-brain hemisphere
  - left-brain functions
- Right-brain hemisphere
  - right-brain functions
- Meditation can lead to an altered state of consciousness associated with right-brain functions

Altered States of Consciousness Characteristics

- Time distortion
- Ineffability
- Present centeredness
- Perception distortion
- Enhanced receptivity
- Self-transcendence

Physiological Effects of Meditation

- Decreased oxygen consumption
- Decreased blood lactate levels
- Increased skin resistance
- Decreased heart rate

Physiological Effects of Meditation
(continued)

- Decreased blood pressure
- Decreased muscle tension
- Increased alpha waves

Psychological Effects of Meditation

- Increased mental acuity
  - (better test scores)
- Increased concentration skills
  - (less ADD)
- Increased emotional stability
  - (less depression)

Meditation and Brain Imaging Research

- Meditation appears to positively alter brain chemistry
- Meditation appears to positively alter neural wiring
- Anyone can adapt to these positive changes by meditation

Meditation and Chronic Pain

- Meditation is often used as a means to decrease chronic pain
- Jon Kabat-Zinn uses mindfulness to treat chronic pain

Steps to Initiate Meditation

- Dedicate a specific time of day
- Dedicate a specific place each time
- Minimize all distractions (e.g., cell phones, TVs, etc.)
- Maintain a comfortable position (keep a straight spine)
- Consider using some type of focusing device (mantra, music, breath)

Best Application of Meditation

- Meditate early in the morning before the day starts for mental clarity
- Meditate before exams or athletic events for mental clarity

Study Guide Questions

1. Explain the difference between inclusive and exclusive meditation and give an example of each.

2. Herbert Benson "Americanized" TM and called it the Relaxation Response. Describe his method.

Notes

_____
_____
_____
_____
_____
_____
_____
_____
_____
_____
_____
_____
_____
_____
_____
_____
_____
_____
_____
_____
_____
_____
_____
_____
_____
_____
_____
_____
_____
_____
_____
_____
_____
_____
_____
_____
_____

Study Guide Questions
(continued)

3. How does the practice of meditation affect the brain?

4. What is an altered state of consciousness?

5. What effects do meditation have on the mind and body?

Notes

Managing Stress
Principles and Strategies for Health and Well-Being

Hatha Yoga

Chapter 19

"The main teaching of yoga is that man's nature is divine."

—Swami Rama

An Historical Perspective of Hatha Yoga

- Introduced thousands of years ago by Pantanjali in ancient India in a book called *The Yoga Sutras*
- Hatha Yoga is one of many types of yoga

Notes

_____
_____
_____
_____
_____
_____
_____
_____
_____
_____
_____
_____
_____
_____
_____
_____
_____
_____
_____
_____
_____
_____
_____
_____
_____
_____
_____
_____
_____
_____
_____
_____
_____
_____
_____

Hatha Yoga

- Yoga is a Sanskrit word meaning "union."
- It refers to the union of mind, body, and spirit.
- Hatha yoga emphasizes physical balance.

Hatha Yoga's Three Premises

- The art of breathing
- The art of conscious stretching
- The art of balance

Physiological Effects of Hatha Yoga

- Offers great means to enhance structural balance
- Relaxes muscles that are tense from stress, poor posture
- When muscles are relaxed, the mind and body become more relaxed
- People report that Hatha Yoga improves quality of sleep

Psychological Effects of Hatha Yoga

- Offers great means to promote mental calmness
- Offers potential for better quality of self-image
- Implicit message of yoga practice maintains a sense of inner peace

Hatha Yoga

- Hatha yoga session will begin with the *namaskar* (Salute to the Sun), which is a series of movements or postures initiating integration of the mind, body, and spirit.
- Asanas are yoga positions
  - moving into the pose
  - maintaining the pose
  - coming out of the pose

Additional Thoughts on Hatha Yoga

- Best not to eat before practice
- Wear loose fitting clothing
- Find a quiet time to practice regularly
- Concentrate on breathing with each asana

Notes

_____
_____
_____
_____
_____
_____
_____
_____
_____
_____
_____
_____
_____
_____
_____
_____
_____
_____
_____
_____
_____
_____
_____
_____
_____
_____
_____
_____
_____
_____
_____
_____

Hatha Yoga and Chronic Pain

- Often prescribed to help with lower back and hip pain (e.g., separation of SI joint)

Best Application of Hatha Yoga

- It's a great way to start or end each day
- Yoga classes help one's motivation to practice
- Keeping muscles *flexible* is a metaphor for life

Study Guide Questions

1. Why is Hatha Yoga thought to be an effective relaxation technique?

2. Explain both the physiological and psychologic effects of Hatha yoga.

3. Hatha Yoga involves three aspects (arts). Please name and explain each.

Notes

Managing Stress
Principles and Strategies
for Health and Well-Being

Mental Imagery and Visualization

Chapter 20

"Imagination is more powerful than knowledge."

—Albert Einstein

An Historical Perspective of Mental Imagery and Visualization

- Origins date back to Freud and Jung in modern psychology
- Most likely used for millennia by people of all cultures
- Shamans used visualization to heal tribe members

Mental Imagery and Visualization

- Mental imagery involves unconscious thoughts that become conscious in the effort to heal or make whole.
- Guided mental imagery is a variation wherein images are suggested by another person.
- Visualization is a conscious thought process directed toward self-improvement.

Mental Imagery Research

- Mental imagery has been the focus of many clinical studies to determine the effectiveness of this technique on many types of illness, most notably cancer. Additional case studies reveal the merits of this approach time and again, where the unconscious mind is invited to actively participate in the healing process.

Mental Imagery as a Relaxation Technique

- Just as real or imaginary thoughts can trigger the stress response, relaxing thoughts can promote the relaxation response.
- When imagination is used to promote relaxation, the body's five senses are in effect deactivated or desensitized to stressful stimuli.

Healing Visualization Tips from Dr. Patricia Norris

- Image must be idiosyncratic
- Image must be egosyntonic
- Image must have a positive aspect
- Image must be kinesthetic and somatic
- Image must be anatomically correct
- Employ constancy and dialogue
- Employ the healthy blueprint aspect
- Employ the treatment with the image

Three Categories of Mental Imagery

- Tranquil natural scenes, or images that place one in a natural environment.
- Behavioral changes, or images that allow one to see and feel oneself performing a different, more health-conscious behavior.
- Internal body images, or images of trips inside the body to observe damaged or diseased tissue being healed or repaired.

Color and Light Therapy

- Research into visualization also includes color and light therapy
  - The color blue appears to have a relaxing/healing effect.
  - Full spectrum lighting is known to have a healing effect too!

Notes

Notes

Mental Imagery and Chronic Pain

- Has been used to identify and alleviate chronic pain, particularly the use of mental imagery and the power of the unconscious mind

Steps to Initiate Mental Imagery and Visualization

- Assume a comfortable position
- Relax (concentrate on breathing)
- Adjust attitude toward receptivity

Steps to Initiate Mental Imagery and Visualization (continued)

- Select a visual theme (beach, forest)
- Allow your mind to enrich the image
- Utilize all the body's senses

Visual Theme for Mental Imagery: Nature Images

Best Application of Mental Imagery

- Mental imagery can be done just about anywhere (before giving a speech, before an exam, falling asleep, etc.)
- A technique that doesn't require much time
- Many Olympic and professional athletes use this technique
- List five situations where this technique would be appropriate
- Pleas, do not use this technique while driving!!!

Study Guide Questions

1. What is mental imagery and how does it differ from visualization?

2. List three categories that imagery and visualization can be used for relaxation.

3. What is color therapy and how can it be used to promote relaxation?

4. List the three steps of guided mental imagery that when followed, help promote relaxation.

Notes

Managing Stress
Principles and Strategies for Health and Well-Being

Music Therapy

Chapter 21

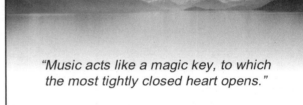

"Music acts like a magic key, to which the most tightly closed heart opens."

—Maria Von Trapp

An Historical Perspective of Music Therapy

- Music as a form of healing is ageless.
- From tribal drumming to medieval court minstrels, every culture has used music for relaxation and healing.
- The expression "music soothes the savage beast" is renowned the world over as a simple truth.
- The National Music Therapy Association was founded in 1950.

Music Therapy

- Music therapy is defined as
  - "the systematic application of music by the music therapist to bring about helpful changes in the emotional or physical health of the client."

  - and the "ability to experience an altered state of physical arousal and subsequent mood by processing a progression of musical notes of varying tone, rhythm, and instrumentation for a pleasing effect."

From Sound to Noise to Music

- Sound is measured in Hertz (Hz)
- Hz measures the vibrations/second
- Sounds are recorded in decibels (dB)
- dB = the air pressure detected by the human ear

The Dynamics of Music*

Tone	Pitch
Intensity	Timbre
Harmony	Interval
Rhythm	Perceptual Quality

*All these factors are involved in music's ability to promote relaxation

Music as a Relaxation Technique

Theories of Music Therapy:
- Biochemical Theory
- Entrainment Theory
- Metaphysical Theory

Music as a Relaxation Technique
(continued)

- The Biochemical Theory states that music is a sensory stimulus that is processed through the sense of hearing. Sound vibrations are chemically changed into nervous impulses that activate either the sympathetic or parasympathetic nervous system.

Music as a Relaxation Technique
(continued)

- The Entrainment Theory, based on a law of physics, suggests that oscillations produced by music are received by the human energy field and the various physiological systems and organs entrain with or resonate with the given Hz (oscillation) of the music.

Music as a Relaxation Technique
(continued)

- The Metaphysical Theory suggests that music and song have a transcending quality that provides a direct communication with the divine.
- Music is divine in nature.
- Many musicians say that when they compose, they are eavesdropping on the thoughts of God (e.g., Mozart, Beethoven, Paul McCartney).

Music Therapy

- For music therapy to be fully effective as a relaxation technique, it is best that the music be instrumental (without lyrics).
- Type of music selected, listening environment, posture, and attitude also affect the quality of the relaxation response.

Physiological Effects of Relaxing Music

- Decreases resting heart rate
- Decreases resting blood pressure
- Decreases muscle tension
- Decreases other metabolic parameters associated with the stress response

Psychological Effects of Music

- Music has a profound ability to effect one's mood whether it's a lullaby or a rock concert

Music Therapy and Chronic Pain

- Two theories:
  1. Music serves as a pleasant distraction from pain
  2. Healing vibrations entrain a healing effect to reduce pain
     - 7.8 Hz is thought to be the vibration of homeostasis
     - Dolphins and whales "sing" at 7.8 Hz

Steps to Initiate Music Therapy

- Make a good musical selection
- Create a good listening environment
- Create your own mix of relaxing songs
  - Select songs without words/lyrics that could engage left brain to run amok with emotions

Notes

_____

_____

_____

_____

_____

_____

_____

_____

_____

_____

_____

_____

_____

_____

_____

_____

_____

_____

_____

_____

_____

_____

_____

_____

_____

_____

_____

_____

_____

_____

_____

_____

_____

_____

_____

_____

_____

Best Application of Music Therapy

- Listening to instrumental music can be a form of meditation
- It should be done without distractions (e.g., cell phones, TVs, etc.)
- Playing an instrument also qualifies as music therapy
- Singing also qualifies as music therapy (so does whistling!)

Study Guide Questions

1. What exactly is music therapy?

2. List and explain the three ways (theories) that music is thought to promote relaxation.

3. Listening to music is one form of music therapy. Name two others.

Chapter 22: Massage Therapy

Notes

Managing Stress
Principles and Strategies
for Health and Well-Being

Massage Therapy

Chapter 22

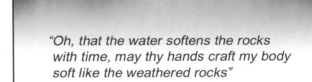

"Oh, that the water softens the rocks with time, may thy hands craft my body soft like the weathered rocks"

—Anonymous

An Historical Perspective of Massage Therapy

Muscle massage is one of the oldest known techniques to relieve stress and muscle tension dating back to Ancient Greece, perhaps further.

Notes

The Need for Human Touch

- Health experts predict that as advances in technology increase (less human contact), so will the need for human touch.
- People tend to get more *anxious* without human touch.
- Increased computer use promotes neck, shoulder and lower back soreness.

Massage Therapy

- Muscle massage is the manipulation of skin, muscles, ligaments, and connective tissue for the purpose of decreasing muscle tension and increasing physical comfort of musculature and its surrounding joints, thereby promoting a deep sense of relaxation.

Massage Therapy
(continued)

- Muscle tension is the number one symptom of stress.
- Muscle massage is one of the oldest known techniques to relieve stress.
- Some researchers believe that our high-tech society increases the need for human touch. Do you?

Massage Therapy
(continued)

- Massage therapy aids in the reduction of muscle tension and provides an essential human need, touch.
- Research shows that massage therapy is as effective in promoting the relaxation response as are other forms of relaxation.

Types of Muscle Massage (Body Work)

- Shiatsu (acupressure)
- Swedish Massage (manipulation, stroking)
- Rolfing (structural integration)
- Myofascial Release (fascial manipulation)
- Sports Massage (deep tissue with Swedish)
- Thai Massage (pulling, lifting limbs, and deep tissue)

Other Touch Therapies

- Hydrotherapy (water therapy, hot tubs, etc.)
- Pet Therapy
- Aromatherapy
- Therapeutic Touch, Healing Touch (Energy Healing)

Massage Therapy and Chronic Pain

- Perhaps more than any other relaxation technique, massage is the preeminent technique to reduce/eliminate muscle/joint pain.

Physiological and Psychological Benefits

- Physical relaxation and decreased muscle tension
- Increased blood supply
- Increased flexibility
- Increased sense of tranquility
- Increased emotional relaxation

Best Application of Massage Therapy

- After prolonged computer office work
- After prolonged physical labor
- After aerobic/anaerobic workouts
- After childbirth for new mothers
- Best technique to reduce muscle tension of any kind

Study Guide Questions

1. What is massage therapy and why is this thought to be an effective means to promote relaxation?

2. List and describe five different styles of massage (body work).

3. What is aromatherapy and why is this technique thought to be relaxing?

Study Guide Questions
(continued)

4. What is hydrotherapy and why is this technique thought to be relaxing?

5. What is pet therapy and why is this technique thought to be relaxing?

Notes

Chapter 23: T'ai Chi Ch'uan

Notes

T'ai Chi Ch'uan

Chapter 23

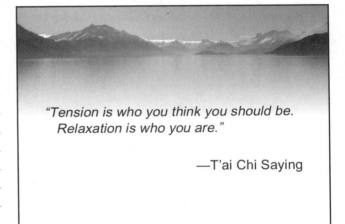

"Tension is who you think you should be. Relaxation is who you are."

—T'ai Chi Saying

Philosophy of T'ai Chi

- The concept of T'ai Chi is based on the philosophy of Taoism, where opposites are brought together in harmony and balance.

T'ai Chi Ch'uan

- To harmonize with the universe, to move in unison with this energy, to move as freely as running water is to be at peace or one with the universe.
- This is the essence of T'ai Chi Ch'uan: a harmony and balance with the vital life force of the natural world itself.

T'ai Chi Ch'uan
(continued)

- The Chinese believe that poor health is a result of blockages and congestion in the flow of internal energy, which in turn lowers one's physical resistance and makes one vulnerable to various pathogens.

T'ai Chi Ch'uan
(continued)

- T'ai Chi is deeply rooted in philosophy, primarily Taoism, but to a lesser extent, Confucianism.
- The premise of this exercise is to move with, rather than against, the flow of universal energy. The positions reinforce the concept of consciously moving with rather than against received stressors in everyday life.

T'ai Chi Ch'uan
Relaxation Technique

- Breathe effortlessly
- Free the body of all tension
- Stand perpendicular to the floor
- Keep your center of gravity low
- Maintain even speed
- Integrate the mind and body as one

Four Principles of T'ai Chi Ch'uan

- Fasting the heart
- Returning to nature
- Wu-wei
- Winning by losing

Physiological Effects of T'ai Chi

- Increased physical stamina
- Increased muscular endurance
- Increased posture
- Decreased bone demineralization

Notes

Notes

_____

_____

_____

_____

_____

_____

_____

_____

_____

_____

_____

_____

_____

_____

_____

_____

_____

_____

_____

_____

_____

_____

_____

_____

_____

_____

_____

_____

_____

_____

_____

_____

_____

Psychological Effects of T'ai Chi

- Increased mental acuity
- Increased concentration skills
- Increased emotional control (balanced emotions)

T'ai Chi and Chronic Pain

By clearing the flow of energy, chi or Qi harmony diminishes the cause of pain.

Best Application of T'ai Chi Ch'uan

- A moving meditation to start or end the day's activities
- When done outside, it helps to reconnect to nature
- A great metaphor for living one's life in balance
- Great for preventing and minimizing osteoporosis

Study Guide Questions

1. T'ai Chi is called a "moving meditation." Explain why.

2. What is the Chi of T'ai Chi?

3. Explain the philosophy of Taoism in simple Western terms as a means to promote relaxation.

4. List/explain both the physiological and psychological effects of T'ai Chi.

Notes

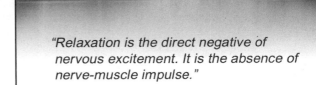

"Relaxation is the direct negative of nervous excitement. It is the absence of nerve-muscle impulse."

—Edmund Jacobson, M.D.

An Historical Perspective of PMR

- Edmund Jacobson was a U.S.-trained physician who noticed that all his patients with illness showed chronic muscle tension. He theorized that if muscle tension was significantly decreased, the chance for illness would diminish.
- PMR has proved to be a popular relaxation technique in the U.S. for many decades.
- It may be the only recognized relaxation technique created in the U.S.

Notes

Progressive Muscular Relaxation

- The body's muscles respond to thoughts of perceived threats with tension or contraction.
- Muscular tension is believed to be the most common symptom of stress, and can lead to:
  - stiffness, pain, discomfort, distorted and disaligned posture, and joint stability.

Progressive Muscular Relaxation
(continued)

- The building blocks involved in muscular contraction are a motor end unit, a motor nerve fiber (neuron), a skeletal muscle fiber, and a stimulus from the nerve fiber to the muscle fiber called an action potential.
- Chemicals released from these neurons are neurotrophic substances.
- Neurotransmitters secrete epinephrine, norepinephrine, and ACh to regulate and control muscle contraction.

Progressive Muscular Relaxation
(continued)

- Muscles can contract in one of three ways:
  - concentrically (shortening)
  - eccentrically (lengthening)
  - isometrically (no visible change in length)
- Muscle tension produced through the stress response is primarily isometric.
- Over time, muscles contracted isometrically can begin to show signs of shortening.

Progressive Muscular Relaxation
(continued)

- Progressive muscular relaxation is a systematic approach to relieving muscle tension.
- Based on the work of Edmund Jacobson, PMR is a simple technique used to promote rest and relaxation by systematically tensing and relaxing the body's musculature, from feet to the head.

Benefits of PMR

- Decreases muscle tension
- As body relaxes, so does the mind
- People who use PMR have less health issues

Steps to Initiate PMR

- Find a comfortable position.
- Begin by monitoring your breathing. Inhale when you contract each muscle group, exhale when you relax each muscle group.
- Focus your concentration on each muscle group as you work various regions of your body.

Notes

Typical Phase for Each Muscle Group Using PMR

- First contraction: 100% @ 5–10 seconds
  - release and relax (exhale)
  - compare relaxation to contraction
- Second contraction: 50% @ 5–10 seconds
  - release and relax (exhale)
  - compare relaxation to contraction
- Third contraction: 5–10% @ 5–10 seconds
  - release and relax (exhale)
  - compare relaxation to contraction

Progressive Muscular Relaxation

- Research indicates that anger elicits the greatest response of unconscious muscle tension. Progressive Muscular Relaxation is one of the best techniques to deal with symptoms of anger.

Best Application of PMR

- Excellent way to reduce muscle tension
- Thought to be beneficial for people who quit smoking
- Avoid using in areas with chronic pain
- Avoid using if you have hypertension

Study Guide Questions

1. Explain the rationale for PMR as an effective relaxation technique.

2. Describe in simple terms how to begin a session of PMR to promote relaxation.

3. What are some conditions where this technique is not advised?

Notes

Managing Stress
Principles and Strategies
for Health and Well-Being

Autogenic Training

Chapter 25

"Open your mind to the power of self-suggestion."

—Johannes Schultz

An Historical Perspective of Autogenic Training

- The creation of Johannes Schultz and Wolfgang Luthe in 1932
- Based on the concept of selective awareness through autosuggestion
- Also called self-regulation by some
- Commonly used in conjunction with clinical biofeedback

Notes

Autogenic Training

- Autogenic training is a technique of self-regulation, whereby individuals are taught to regulate various aspects of their body's physiology, specifically the flow of blood to a specific region of the body to make that area feel warm and heavy.

Autogenic training is effective when:

- The individual is highly motivated and receptive to instructions and suggestions.
- The individual possesses a strong sense of self-direction and control.
- The individual positions him or herself comfortably.

Autogenic training is effective when: (continued)

- The individual maintains a strong sense of concentration and body awareness.
- The individual minimizes sensory reception.
- The individual focuses on internal physiological processes.

Autogenic Training

- *Selective awareness* is a term used to explain how the mind focuses attention on the self-suggestion and receptivity that produce a sense of relaxation.
- *Autogenic discharge* refers to various sensory sensations and emotional responses triggered by autogenic training.

Two General Approaches to Autogenic Training

- Direct method: The person consciously moves blood to the extremities where warmth and heaviness are desired.
- Indirect method: The person focuses only on warmth and heaviness, not blood flow.

Best Application of Autogenic Training

- Autogenics is portable, it can be done anywhere (home, office, etc.)
- A great technique to use to fall asleep for people with insomnia
- A great technique used in surgery to minimize complications

Notes

Notes

_____
_____
_____
_____
_____
_____
_____
_____
_____
_____
_____
_____
_____
_____
_____
_____
_____
_____
_____
_____
_____
_____
_____
_____
_____
_____
_____
_____
_____
_____
_____
_____
_____
_____
_____
_____
_____
_____
_____
_____

Study Guide Questions

1. Explain the rationale for autogenics as a relaxation technique.

2. Describe in simplest terms how to do autogenics as a technique to promote relaxation.

Notes

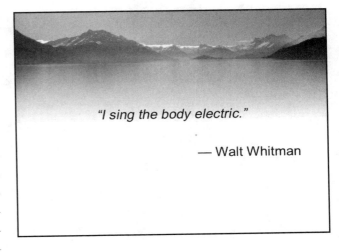

An Historical Perspective of Biofeedback

- Biofeedback is a technique that gained popularity in the late 1960s
- Most people's exposure to biofeedback is from polygraph tests shown on television shows

Biofeedback

- Biofeedback is a process of gathering information about specific physiological functions such as:
  - heart rate
  - respiration
  - body temperature

Clinical Biofeedback

- Clinical biofeedback is the use of monitoring instruments to amplify the electrochemical energy produced by various body organs.

Clinical Biofeedback
(continued)

- Clinical biofeedback allows a person to increase awareness of his or her own physiological responses by learning to monitor them through data gathered by a particular instrument.

Clinical Biofeedback
(continued)

- The purpose of biofeedback is to teach people with stress-related disorders to recondition their responses so that they gain control over the physiological system responsible for their symptoms.

The Biofeedback Loop

Sensors

Detection, Amplification

Signal conditioning

Person

Program logic

Recording

Feedback

Feedback signal processing

Auditory - variety of sounds
Visual - numbers, meters, lights

Biofeedback

- Biofeedback teaches people how to monitor and change the frequency and amplitude of the electronic signals by controlling (relaxing) the body region to which the electrodes are attached. The three phases of biofeedback are:
  - Awareness of physiological response
  - Control of physiological response
  - Application of reconditioned response in everyday routines

Clinical Biofeedback

- Clinical biofeedback, to strengthen the conditioned response, combines sophisticated technology and various other forms of relaxation, including:
- diaphragmatic breathing
- autogenic training
- progressive muscular relaxation
- mental imagery

Clinical Biofeedback
(continued)

- There are several types of clinical biofeedback, each monitoring a specific physiological system; these are:
- electromyography (EMG)
- electroencephalography (EEG)
- electrocardiography (EKG)
- electro dermal (EDR)

Best Application of Biofeedback

- To learn to reduce chronic pain of:
  - Headaches
  - Stomach cramps
  - IBS
  - Colitis
  - Back pain
  - Raynaud's disease
  - Insomnia

Study Guide Questions

1. Explain the rationale for biofeedback as an effective relaxation technique.

2. Explain three different types of biofeedback.

3. List five health conditions that could possibly be improved with the use of biofeedback.

Notes

Notes

Nutrition and Stress

Chapter 27

"Fortunately or unfortunately, we live in a world that tempts us with a great variety and abundance of food, and many of us eat not to satisfy physical hunger, but to allay anxiety, depression, and boredom, to provide a substitute for emotional nourishment, or to try to fill an inner void."

—Andy Weil, M.D.

Nutrition and Stress

- First and foremost, food is a pacifier
- People eat to calm their emotions (fear and/or anger)

Notes

Optimal Nutrition Includes:

- Nutrients
- Digestion
- Absorption
- Metabolism
- Elimination

Nutritional Recommendations

- Nutritionists recommend that you follow guidelines regarding:
  - adequacy (of essential nutrients)
  - moderation (limited sugar, fat, and salt)
  - balance (of nutrients), caloric control, and variety

Six Essential Nutrients

- Carbohydrates
- Fats
- Proteins
- Vitamins
- Minerals
- Water

A Malnourished Diet

- A malnourished diet—one that is deficient of essential amino acids, essential fats, vitamins, and minerals—is itself a stressor on the body.

Poor Nutrition and Stress

- Research has shown that some foods actually induce a state of stress. Excess amounts of sugar, caffeine, salt, bleached flour, and foods poor in vitamins and minerals weaken the body's resistance to the stress response.

Additional Stress and Nutritional Factors

- A high-fat diet suppresses the immune system
- Excess simple sugars deplete vitamin stores, particularly B-complex
- Caffeine triggers sympathetic nervous system
- Chronic stress depletes vitamins B & C

Notes

Additional Stress and Nutritional Factors (continued)

- High sodium may raise blood pressure
- Excessive alcohol consumption is thought to suppress the immune system
- Hydrogenated and partially hydro-genated foods = trans fatty acids, leading to free radical damage to cells

---

Nutritional Needs of Women

- Women should pay specific attention to their nutritional needs regarding the relationship between food substances and:
  - breast soreness
  - breast cancer
  - cervical cancer
  - colorectal cancer
  - premenstrual problems
  - osteoporosis

Eating Disorders

- Anorexia
- Bulimia
- Overeating

Nutrition and the Immune System

- Food can either enhance or suppress the immune system.
- Most foods today are laden with toxic chemicals that tax the immune system. Stress only compounds the problem.
- If you are susceptible to disease or illness, or have a disease or illness follow the advice of Hippocrates:
  - "Let food be your medicine and let medicine be your food."

Nutrition and the Immune System I

- Consume bountiful antioxidants
- Consume healthy amounts of fiber
- Drink adequate amounts of clean filtered water
- Consume adequate amounts of protein
- Decrease processed foods and junk food
- Decrease the synthetic pesticides, herbicides, fungicides, and fertilizers in food

Nutrition and the Immune System II

- Decrease antibiotics and hormones in food
- Consume a healthy balance of omega 3's & 6's
- Decrease the consumption of saturated fats
- Eliminate consumption of trans fatty acids
- Consume healthy amounts of bioflavinoids
- Consume healthy foods with pH balance

Notes

Notes

Nutrition and the Immune System III

- Replace nutrients depleted from stress
- Decrease consumption of processed sugars
- Eliminate aspartame and MSG (excitotoxins)
- Prepare food in the best way possible (e.g., steam veggies instead of microwaving them)
- Consume organic foods whenever possible
- Avoid all GMOs (frankenfoods)
- Use herbal therapies that boost the immune system

Recapping the Stress-Nutrition-Disease Domino Effect

- Stress can deplete the body of much needed essential nutrients
- Good eating habits are nonexistent when people are stressed (nutrients are not replaced!)
- Some foods/beverages act as gasoline on the fires of stress
- Additives, preservatives, synthetic chemicals tax the immune system
- The body's immune system is ill prepared to combat invading forces
- Acute and or chronic illness occurs in a vacuum of a poor immune system.

Study Guide Questions

1. How does stress affect one's eating habits?

2. How does stress affect digestion, absorption, and elimination?

3. How does stress affect the body's use of nutrients?

4. What foods are known to trigger the stress response?

Study Guide Questions
(continued)

5. List three recommendations for healthy nutrition.

6. List five recommendations to boost your immune system through good nutritional practices.

7. How do herbs help promote homeostasis?

Notes

Notes

Managing Stress
Principles and Strategies
for Health and Well-Being

Physical Exercise

Chapter 28

"A sound mind in a sound body."

—Juvenal

Physical Exercise

- Physical exercise is a form of stress; the enactment of all the physiological systems that the fight-or-flight response triggers for physical survival.

Physical Exercise
(continued)

- Physical exercise is a very effective means to reduce stress and a most natural means to express the manifestation of the stress response.

Physical Exercise
(continued)

- Anaerobic (without oxygen) is short, intense, and powerful activity.
- Aerobic (with oxygen) is moderately intense activity for a prolonged period of time.

Physiological Effects of Physical Exercise

- Decreased resting heart rate
- Decreased resting blood pressure
- Decreased muscle tension
- Better quality sleep
- Increased resistance to colds and illness
- Increased tolerance of heat and cold through acclimatization

Physiological Effects of Physical Exercise (continued)

- Decreased serum levels of cholesterol and triglycerides
- Decreased percent of body fat (improved body composition)
- Increased efficiency of heart muscle
- Decreased bone demineralization
- Decreased rate of aging
- Greater sense of overall well-being

Physical Exercise, Stress, and Balance

- Physical exercise may be a stress to the body, but in moderate amounts, it tends to regulate (balance) the body's physiological functions.
- Homeostasis is regained through "parasympathetic rebound."

Theory of Athletic Conditioning: All or None Principle

intensity   frequency

duration   mode

Phases of a Workout

- Warm-up period (5–10 minutes)

- Stimulus period (20–30 minutes)

- Cool-down period (5–10 minutes)

Phases of a Workout

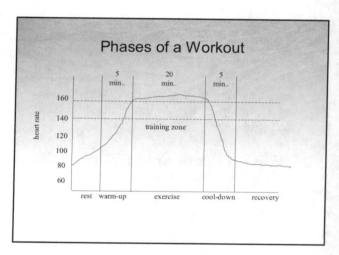

Psychological Effects of Physical Exercise

- Improved self-esteem
- Improved sense of self-reliance, self-efficacy
- Improved mental alertness, perception, and information processing

Psychological Effects of Physical Exercise
(continued)

- Increased perceptions of acceptance by others
- Decreased feelings of depression and anxiety
- Decreased overall sense of stress and tension

Steps to Initiate a Fitness Training Program

- Start cautiously, progress moderately
- Pick an activity that you really enjoy
- Select a time of day to exercise
- Exercise using the right clothes and equipment

Steps to Initiate a Fitness Training Program
(continued)

- For motivation, work out with friends
- Set personal fitness goals for yourself
- Take precautions, avoid injuries

Notes

Notes

Exercise and Chronic Pain

- Overuse syndrome can promote pain
- Pilates is used by many to reduce symptoms of lower back pain

Best Application of Physical Exercise

- Be sure to get an adequate warm-up and cool-down
- Be sure to exercise at the right intensity, frequency, and duration
- Never underestimate the benefits of walking
- Exercise helps to flush out stress hormones
- Parasympathetic rebound promotes a healthy sense of homeostasis
- Physical exercise allows for the release of pent up emotions too!

Study Guide Questions

1. Explain how physical exercise is "stress," but also helps to reduce stress.

2. How does anaerobic exercise differ from aerobic exercise?

3. List five physiological effects of cardiovascular exercise training.

4. List and explain the proven steps to begin and continue a successful exercise program.